How to Live Your Faith

How to Live Your Faith

Missional Members Work for a More Loving and More Just World with God's Help

A. WAYNE SCHWAB

VTS PRESS
Alexandria, Virginia
2022

VTS PRESS

Virginia Theological Seminary
3737 Seminary Road
Alexandria, VA 22304
www.vts.edu

ISBN: 979-8-4230-5785-5

All proceeds from this book will go to support the mission
of Virginia Theological Seminary.

Contents

Guideposts

Preface and Acknowledgements

This book represents the culmination of my life's work as an Episcopal priest in finding God, helping others to find God, and most importantly, helping us all to fulfill what I believe to be God's primary mission in the world, which is to bring love and justice to every situation.

A brief summary of my personal journey that has led to my process for training missional members is found in the first chapter of this book. I have written two previous books on the topic of missional members.

My first book, *When the Members are the Missionaries: An Extraordinary Calling for Ordinary People,* published in 2002, lays out in detail the seven primary mission fields in everyone's life and details a way to introduce this process for missional membership to a congregation. You will find many actual stories of people bringing love and justice to the world, and gain insights into how they came to understand that they can live and work with God in every part of their daily lives.

My second book, *Living the Gospel: A Guide for Individuals and Small Groups,* co-authored by my daughter, Elizabeth S. Hall, is a companion piece to the first book. It can be used as a workbook to jumpstart an individual or group effort to get a clearer sense of what God is calling them to do in every part of their daily lives, while recognizing and receiving the help and companionship with God needed to carry on their missions.

This book, *How to Live Your Faith*, provides a step-by-step process for a church leader to understand and live missional membership, and then how to transform a congregation by making missional membership the center of the church's mission.

Many individuals have helped me in my life's journey, which is expressed throughout this book, but I would like to name those most important to this current work. I have treasured the input, support, and wisdom of my "team of four" who acted as consultants: Robert D. Hughes, Ann P. Lynch, Demi Prentiss, and Rev. Craig Smith. I am thankful for the following individuals who helped bring my words into focus as editors: Ann Barker, Catharine S. June, and Rev. Samantha Ruth Elizabeth Smith. And finally, I would like to acknowledge that I could not have completed this work without the love and support of my late wife of 54 years, Elizabeth P. Schwab, and my wife of 10 years today, Renate Parke, and my four children: Stephen W. Schwab, Burton P. Schwab, Catharine S. June, and Elizabeth S. Hall.

Introduction

In This Chapter

Who can use this book? • A resume of my journey to "missional members" • The world's need for missions of love and justice • The pages ahead

Who can use this book?

This book is for clergy and visionary lay leaders skilled in leading others into fresh ways of living their faith. They will develop the vision and the methods to form congregations of missional members, members who believe they are on God's mission to make the world more loving and more just wherever they are. They will also find a workshop to train members to find their own missions as part of God's mission.

Many more can use it as well. Church members who catch the missional member vision can give this book to leaders whom they believe are open to catching it as well. Seminary faculty and judicatory leaders and their staffs can use this book to orient clergy and lay leaders to a future that is coming where the primary emphasis is on living the faith. Non-members, even atheists, can be reached through the approach taken in this book.

How I came to "missional members" and this book

During my time on the staff of the Presiding Bishop of the Episcopal Church, 1975-93, and in retirement, my interest in what church members were doing to make the world a better place kept growing and growing. I began to ask, "How does your faith connect with what you are doing?" or "Do you see God at work in any way in what you are doing?" I was excited not only by what they were doing but how easily they told me how they saw their faith and God connected with what they were doing.

Reading about a missionary spirituality[1] gave me a next step in putting together what church members can do to create a better world. I was hearing about missions – about what members were doing with God's help to make the world a better place. Making the world a better place had become the best way I knew to describe what God was and is doing. The members were telling me how their missions are part of God's mission.

I started creating various documents to help members to live and talk about their missions. The more I used them, the more excited members became about the connections they were making. Together we were discovering that all of us were on mission without knowing it. We were living a missionary spirituality already. Already we had purpose and power for life. We were already members on mission in every part of daily life.

Already, we are missional members. All church members are missional. Many of us do not see what we are doing as part of God's mission already. So, it is time to write about missional members and to help us all see the big picture of God's mission in the world and how we are already living it.

My life has prepared me for this discovery and for writing about it. Some of the formative experiences that brought me here are:

- seminary, college, church, and home which made love and justice my primary values;
- a brief year selling door-to-door which introduced me to the business world;
- two years developing 5th and 6th grade church school curriculum as assistant rector collaborating with the Christian education director and two volunteer teachers;
- nineteen years leading a growing church that called for strong teamwork with the members;

---

[1] Brian Farran's report of the qualities of effective congregations in Western Australia in the Anglican Theological Review, Fall 1996.

- training in human relationships, communication, small group life, and organizational development that continue to enable all I do;
- therapy that enabled growth to make marriage and family life and church life and leadership better;
- an interfaith community service project and work with the National Council of Churches that brought needed insights and friendships;
- ability to use non-theological language in talking about God and the church which came through reading[2] and through seminars of the World Council of Churches and touring European lay academies;
- nineteen years as the first evangelism staff person for the Episcopal Church which led me into every diocese stateside and seven countries in Central and South America, Europe, and Asia;
- working with lay and clergy consultants around the world that increased flexibility on both church and social issues;[3]

---

[2] Especially, Paul Van Buren's *The Secular Meaning of the Gospel: Based on an Analysis of its Language* (Macmillan, 1963). Other examples are the German Lay Academies founded after World War II to rebuild Germany along Christian lines. The academies regularly gathered all related to a given social issue to find a resolution together. Held in church-sponsored centers, each conference included a theological input in non-theological language. For example, at Bad Boll Academy near Stuttgart, a conference for planners received a talk entitled "The Future is Open."

[3] One was Mark Gibbs who as chair of the Leaders' Circle of the European Lay Academies in the 1960s introduced me to these unique institutions. He also co-authored *God's Frozen People* (Fontana Press, 1968). Gibbs was a frequent visitor in my national church office, 1975-1993, keeping me focused on mission rather than the institution. Another was James D. Anderson who co-authored *The Management of Ministry* (Harper & Row, 1978,1990); who served as mission developer in the Diocese of Washington (1973-80); who, with me, led workshops for finding one's mission in one's retirement years (1990-1993); and who consults all levels of church life.

- being funded by Trinity Church of New York City for research in 25 small churches from New Jersey to Alaska which affirmed the ability of congregations to support their members in living their daily missions, in living as the missional members they are;
- in retirement, collecting and reporting in a newsletter the experiences of laity making the world a better place;
- and, also in retirement from 1993 on, I was able to continue developing the insights and procedures of missional membership that inform this book.

The world needs members on missions of love and justice

I believe that our primary purpose in creation is to build a more loving and just world with God's help. We are well on our way. Humankind is blessed with people who seek to lead us towards more loving and just ways of living, people who are trying to make the world a better place by enfranchising voters, creating innovative health care solutions, caring for our planet, and protecting the vulnerable.

We need more members on mission who work to make the world a more loving and just place day in and day out wherever they are. We need people for whom love does not give way to me-first and justice does not give way to our-crowd-first mentalities. Working for love and justice requires committed long-distance runners. Long distance runners need stamina and conviction.

Members on mission run the distance and do it with God's help at every step. The world needs as many members on mission as it can get.

Leaders, clergy and lay, this is the challenge: to connect with and support all church members as part of God's mission to make the world more loving and more just for us, for future generations, and for our planet – all with God's help.

The pages ahead

This book is designed to walk you through the process of cultivating missional members in your congregation. You will find real world examples and helpful procedures and resources throughout the chapters that follow. You will also find many learning activities and worksheets. Some of them are suggested in the list below.

- A revelation of the heart of being a missional member – Chapter 1

- Steps for you as pastor or leader to understand being a missional member – Chapter 1

- Two ways that you as pastor or leader can make an early start in forming missional members – Chapter 1

- Hints to open your ears to hear the missions of members when they come to you – Chapter 2

- Steps for you as pastor or leader to discern your seven missions – Chapter 3

- Steps for you as pastor to awaken the official board to being missional members with a four-session workshop – Chapters 4, 5, 6 and 7

- Seven examples of members discerning their missions – Chapter 8

- Steps to spread the member mission vision throughout your congregation, to choose a way for your congregation to serve its community, and to help your members to live their missions in the wider world – Chapter 9

- Some elements of the spirituality of missional members – Chapter 10

1

The heart of being a missional member is working for love and justice

Begin with the foundational unit of a missional church: the missional member

A missional member is the foundational unit of a missional church. A missional member can be defined as someone who accepts the call to be part of God's mission. The premise of this book is that God's mission is to make every part of one's daily life more loving and more just.

The characteristics of being a member on mission include the following:

- We are baptized, and called to join Jesus' mission to make the world more loving and more just.
- We identify that there is at least one specific mission involved in each of our Seven Mission Fields, described below.
- We recognize that Church on Sunday guides and empowers us for living our missions Monday to Saturday.
- This changes everything for many people. "Church work" under the church's roof becomes only one part of our mission work under God's roof.
- Church members become missional members as they work to make the world more loving and more just.

Our Seven Mission Fields are:[1]

1. home (all in the home and close friends);
2. work (includes home management, school, and volunteer work);
3. community (neighborhood, town, or city);
4. wider world (from social norms to voluntary, business, or governmental systems);
5. leisure (whatever rests or refreshes you);
6. spiritual health (your inner life with God); and
7. church life and outreach (your part in your church's life and outreach at any level).

The mission fields

The source of the mission fields is Martin Luther, who wrote specifically about home, work, the community, and the church. Life in today's world calls for us to make explicit the wider world from social norms to systems. Emphasis on more free time calls for explicit focus on leisure, and increased attention to spirituality calls for explicit attention to spiritual health.

God is on mission in each area or field of daily life. Each missional member discerns what God is doing in each area or field to make life there more loving and just. Next, each decides how to join what God is already doing there. That choice becomes each person's current mission in that field. At any given moment, each has seven missions, one for each mission field. In actual practice, each of us carries on one to three missions in a given day. For the average person, missions at home and at work take up five days of each week. A third mission, community or wider world, usually joins these two during those five days. Weekends often center on leisure, spiritual health, and church. What God is doing and when and

---

[1] A mission field is one of the areas of daily life which we, with God's help, seek to make more loving and/or more just as part of God's mission.

how you join what God is already doing have infinite combinations.

Actually, missions in the seven fields abound in both the Hebrew and Christian bibles. The *home* life of Ruth led her to choose to stay with Naomi and become an ancestor of David (Ruth 1:15-18 and 4:13-17). Exploitation of the poor called Micah, the prophet, to challenge Israel to "do justice and to love mercy" in the *wider world* of the nation (Micah 6:8). In spite of fierce opposition within and without, Nehemiah led the rebuilding of the walls and gates of the vulnerable, remnant *community* of Jews in Jerusalem and he did it in fifty-two days (Nehemiah 6:15-16). The Syro-Phoenician woman provides us with an example of someone who will go to great lengths to secure the spiritual well-being of others (Mark 7:24-30). The *church life and outreach* of the first Christians drew others in through the quality of their shared life together (Acts 2:43-47). Needing to support himself in Corinth, Paul resumed skill as a tent-maker to *work* with Aquila, already a tent-maker, and became both a friend and co-worker with Aquila and his wife, Priscilla, in spreading the Gospel (Acts 18:1-3 and Romans 16:3). Stories of mission in *leisure* time are found in the many accounts of Jesus dining with others (begin with Mark 2:15).

Love and justice are at the heart of the biblical accounts of God's words and works

Love and justice are signs of God's presence among us. Love and justice are the center of God's mission and of our own missions. They help us to find where God is on mission and to find our own missions within God's mission.

Wherever you find love and justice, God is present and at work. Wherever the two are weak or absent, God is already there working to restore them. Love and justice have guided the biblical writers from the first. They guide us in finding our missions as well. Both testaments abound in love and justice.

God's love

After crossing the Red Sea to escape Pharaoh's oppression (c. 1290 BCE), Moses and the people sing, "In your steadfast love you led the people you redeemed, you guided them by your strength to your holy abode" (Exodus 15:13). In spite of oppression of the poor, personal immorality, and worship of false gods, God does not give up loving Israel. Hosea (c. 745 BCE) understands God to be saying, "How can I give you up, Ephraim? How can I hand you over, O Israel? . . . I will not execute my fierce anger; . . . for I am God and no mortal" (Hosea 11:8-9).

Jesus sums up the law and the prophets saying, "'You shall love the Lord your God with all your heart, and with all your soul, and with all your mind.' This is the greatest and first commandment. And a second is like it: 'You shall love your neighbor as yourself'" (Matthew 22:37-39). Enemies are to be loved as well: "Love your enemies and pray for those who persecute you" (Matthew 5:44).

God's justice

Amos (c. 760 BCE) sees the people worshiping outwardly with little amendment of life the next day; and the poor selling themselves into slavery to buy shoes for their children (Amos 8:5-6). He senses God saying: "I hate, I despise your festivals, and I take no delight in your solemn assemblies. . . But let justice roll down like waters, and righteousness like an ever-flowing stream" (Amos 5:21-24). Micah (c. 730 BCE), surrounded by greed, lack of justice for the poor, and apostasy, calls for change: "What does the Lord require of you but to do justice, and to love kindness, and to walk humbly with your God?" (Micah 6:8).

Early in his ministry, Jesus goes to the synagogue in Nazareth "as was his custom." He stands to read, is given the scroll of Isaiah, and chooses Isaiah 4:18: "The Spirit of the Lord is upon me, because he has anointed me to bring good news to the poor . . . to proclaim release to the captives . . . to let the oppressed go free." With the eyes of all centered on him, he says, "Today this scripture has been fulfilled in your hearing" (Luke 4:16-21).

Jesus' death and resurrection are the ultimate confrontation with injustice. Injustice is overcome with God's justice. The resurrection proclaims the only just one is the one on the cross. Pilate, the crowd, the disciples – yea, all of us – are the unjust. Yet while the cross declares the injustice of all of us, the resurrection proclaims the justice God. God overcomes injustice and gives us power to cope with injustice in ourselves and others. As Jesus is raised to life, so are we raised with him to new life. The final word is not our injustice but the justice and love of God. ". . . this man you crucified . . . God raised him up . . ." (Acts 2:23-24). "God . . . made us alive together with Christ and raised us up with him" (Ephesians 2:4-6). Even when the doors are locked, Jesus appears and says, "'As the Father has sent me, so I send you.' When he had said this, he breathed on them and said to them, 'Receive the Holy Spirit'" (John 20:21-22).

Today, we use love and justice in many ways. This book works from a contemporary description of love and justice that can help you to discern signs of God's presence in your life and in today's world. It can also help you to discern your own daily missions as part of God's mission.

1. Love is seeking, without limit, to value others as they really are, to care for them, to forgive their faults, and to help them put their skills and talents to their best possible use.

2. Justice is the "public" face of love. In public life, we love by seeking for everyone equal access to food, housing, just wages, health care, education and whatever else helps them to become all that they are created to be and to put their skills and talents to their best possible use.

Five characteristics of a mission

Each mission is centered in love and justice.

Some missions are deeds. Some are words. Some combine deed and word. Without the presence of love or justice, an action fails to be a mission. Will your mission improve the daily lives of the people involved? In our personal lives, we love face-to-face. In our public life, we love by being just.

Missions are specific.

Each mission calls for specifics in what you do or say. A home-builder is on mission to use the design and materials that the client wants and can afford. An elected office-holder is on mission to talk with her constituents as a peer, not as a superior. A teacher is on mission to know his material and to present it clearly.

Missions are costly.

Missions cost in time and energy. Jesus alerted his followers to this fact when He said. "If any want to become my followers, let them deny themselves and take up their cross and follow me" (Mark 8:34).

Making a loving relationship work, parenting with sensitivity, increasing your competence at work, and voting as an informed citizen are costly missions. Missions can call for risk-taking as well. A resident taking on a mission to support low-income housing in her neighborhood risks having to cope with the anger of neighbors. A youth leader at his church risks stressing his family by taking time to chaperone a mission trip for the youth group.

Jesus also cautioned his followers when he said, "Foxes have holes, and birds of the air have nests; but the Son of Man has nowhere to lay his head" (Luke 9:58).

Missions can lead to the conflict and pain of confronting and seeking to correct wrongs. A parent takes on his or her teen's anger by repeatedly calling for healthy, life-preserving values over what can be only passing trends. Whistle-blowers can lose their jobs when they tell the truth about some abuse in the system, the business, or the government agency they serve. In such moments, we are tempted to give up confrontation and correction and to withdraw into forgiveness and acceptance of what is as beyond any hope of change. To say to oneself, "Let it be," can be self-protection rather than wisdom.

Missions need God's help.

Our capacity to bring greater love and justice into the world by ourselves is limited. The love or caring that a situation or person needs can drain our energy. Broken people or situations can drain our energy even more quickly. Wrong-doing by people can tax our forgiveness. Further, the best of our intentions and actions can be infected with self-serving or self-righteousness, or both. We need God's help to keep us focused on the needs of others rather than on our own needs.

Missions satisfy us as we share in God's mission.

We see what we are doing bear fruit as love and justice grow. When there is little or no response or progress, we need to trust that God's love or justice will prevail in the long run. Parenting requires patience because the results are long in coming. Social service is slow to bear fruit as well. People in elected office learn to make change one step at a time. Always, our trust is in God to prevail. Missions carry the special reward of the peace "which surpasses all understanding" (Philippians 4:7) because we trust God to overcome some day.

What missional members will do

Missional members have a wide sphere of influence on others, including:

The congregation

Missional members go into the world to live out their missions wherever they are. Their example leads all of the members to seek to do the same. The congregation rejoices to see growing fulfillment of the promises of baptism in daily life.

The members themselves

Missional members affirm that everything members do to make the world more loving and more just is known and valued by God. Everything from preparing food and doing the dishes to being leaders in Congress is recognized and treasured by God. Members are recognized for already living lovingly and justly as full partners in God's mission.

Church leaders

Leaders are free to ask members for help. They ask without apology for taking members' time and energy. Members hear requests for help as calls to share in mission.

The world

All who, in various ways, are working for a more loving and just world will be strengthened by the missional members who add their will and energy to the various works under way or who will lead others into new works for a better world.

Missional living means more than church work

At best, by "church work" we usually mean deeds or words that include being loving and just, being specific, bearing their cost, and sensing they are done with God's help. They do have a unique characteristic. They are all done in church facilities or as part of church-sponsored programs. Thus, "church work" includes everything from teaching Sunday School to belonging to a youth group to serving on the finance committee. We readily call these deeds or words "church," "mission," or "Christian."

However, deeds or words done or spoken apart from church facilities or church-sponsored programs may bear these five marks but still be seen as second-class. We call them "good works," but we do not speak of them as "church," "mission," or "Christian."

Missional members do all of the above without labelling their work as either "church work" or "good works." Instead, we call the work either missional living or the work of missional members.

All mission comes to us from God, the source of all mission

The heart of mission is God's mission. God is on mission to make the world – at least, this part of the universe –more loving and more just. Read the Bible as the story of God getting across to us that a loving and just world is the world God wants. Freed from Pharaoh, Israel receives the Ten Commandments – God's call to loving and just living – at Mount Sinai. In the passage of time, the ten become the two commandments to love God and to love your neighbor. The prophets get across loving your neighbor as seeking justice for your neighbor and not just for yourself. Both love and justice are what God wants from us. Jesus, empowered by the Spirit, lives that way. His death proclaims how hard, how costly love and justice are. Risen and made known in the breaking of bread, his Spirit feeds and empowers our love and justice. While we still have a long way to go, we make every new step with God's help.

God's mission is building a more loving and just world. God calls each of us to be part of God's mission. God is the source and the enabler of our growth as missional members.

It is from God's mission and Spirit at work in us that our own growth as missional members comes.[2]

Missional members live the Gospel

From the beginning, this book has been guided by these two truths of mission:

1. God is on mission to make the world more loving and more just.
2. We join God's mission to make the world more loving and more just with God's help.

Members on mission live the Gospel. Jesus proclaims the Gospel in Mark 1:15: "The time is fulfilled, and the kingdom of God has come near; repent, and believe in the good news."

Evil is real; it must be overcome. Jesus fulfills the assurance of the prophets that God would intervene decisively one day. In Jesus, God has come in fullness to overcome evil. Jesus is God's agent to overcome evil. The final truth about Jesus is not the suffering servant; Jesus overcomes evil in his resurrection.[3]

Missional members take on the careless and the unjust as they work to overcome evil and to make the world more loving and more just. Missional members join Jesus' mission of love and justice to overcome evil in every part of their daily lives with God's help.

Missional members
and partly-missional churches

Many congregations are recovering their call to serve their communities as part of their call to follow Jesus and to be part of God's mission. They are known as "missional

---

[2] For more on God's Spirit at work in us, see Chapter 10.
[3] "Christus victor" was Gustav Aulen's term (*Christus Victor*, Macmillan, 1931) for Jesus the victor over evil.

churches." Their activities vary from food shelves for the hungry to hostels for homeless young people. These and similar ministries are substantive ways for churches to say to their communities, "We want to be among your loving, justice-building friends." Members take on roles in these community services as part of their mission field of their church and its outreach.

The truth about "missional churches" is that they are only partly missional. Taking a second look at missional churches, we properly ask each missional church if it is missional enough. Members sharing in the community service of their church are meeting the outreach half of the mission field of church and its outreach. However, we must ask how many of the members are actually part of their church's community ministry year-round? A usual answer is about 10%. Such a church is only partly missional.

Church members may be part of the volunteer fire department, serve as first responders, serve on local boards, or lead home and school organizations. Such members are seldom celebrated by their congregations; neither do congregations encourage such involvement. They are not "church work." As part of their work, fully missional churches support, encourage, and celebrate what members do on their own.

Further, to move beyond being partly-missional, each church starts to offer programs and activities that support members in the other six mission fields. A Saturday workshop with a family counselor for teens helps parents in their mission of home and friends. A church that calls a member who is a skilled computer guru to offer a workshop for beginners is supporting missions in daily work. To be more fully missional in the wider world, a church's outreach task force makes viewing and discussion of Al Gore's *An Inconvenient Sequel: Truth to Power* open to all members and makes a brief summary available for all who did not participate.

Still further, state and national issues arise in the seven fields of mission. Ways for members to act on issues of gerrymandering and restricted hours for voting are in the mission fields of both the community and the wider world. Further still, devotional helps for Advent and Lent sent to all of a church's members are part the field of spiritual health. These and similar events move a church beyond being only partly missional.

These are only suggestions of how churches can be more fully missional. This huge field of fully missional churches needs fuller discussion throughout the whole Christian church.

Our focus now turns to leading missional members.

Your steps to leading missional members

1. Listen to and value the missions you see and hear that are grounded in the missional member vision and approach.
2. Update your official board on your interest and development in missional membership and ways you may be practicing it already. Lead them through a workshop orienting them to being missional members by meeting and completing mission discernment forms. For more on these forms, see Chapter 3.
3. In all you do, draw on missional member insights in teaching, preaching, pastoral or mutual care, and spiritual formation.
4. Work out a mission statement with the board that centers on supporting the daily missions of the members.
5. Begin to orient all leaders to missional membership and ask them to spread it among the groups they lead and with all they know throughout the whole congregation.
6. Begin to connect with individuals and groups in the community and wider world as you seek ways for the church you lead and for you as an individual to make life more loving and more just.
7. With the board, develop ways to maintain the growth of missional members throughout the congregation.

Missional membership helps both leaders and members every day

There are benefits to both leaders and members who use the missional member model in everyday ministry. We define a "leader" as any clergy or lay person charged with the responsibility to develop missional initiatives in a congregation; and we see as a "missional member" any one of all of the baptized. When anyone is baptized, he or she joins God's mission in Jesus Christ.

Leaders find leading is easier and more satisfying

Leaders, both ordained and lay, rejoice to find that their work for and with missional members combines pastoral care, teaching and spiritual formation together. Spirituality becomes involved in the first question to ask when you look for your mission in any of the seven mission fields – e.g., "What has God been doing in . . . (this mission field)?" The central place of love and justice in missional living calls for teaching their basis in both the individual and social narratives of the Bible. All dimensions of pastoral care are opened up by the way missional living requires face-to-face conversation about the issues of personal and public life.

When the members have the missional mind-set, leaders are not "laying something on" the members; rather, they are connecting with and supporting what the members are already doing.

Leaders find that working with and teaching about missional membership puts teaching, pastoral care, and spiritual formation together.

Leaders discover they live in constant relationship and dialog with God. The Spirit is helping them to see the kinds of activities God wants from them and the Spirit is helping them to do them.

Both leaders and members find release from past patterns to now work together with deeper mutual affirmation and empowerment as the equals they are.

Missional members find church life more satisfying

Members are both reassured and delighted to see their daily missions recognized, celebrated, and supported.

Members discover they live in constant relationship and dialog with God. The Spirit is helping them to see what God may be wanting them to do and helping them to do it.

Differences, even conflicts, are easier to resolve since everyone is walking on the same street, i.e., everyone is committed to the same mission of making the world more loving and more just.

Responsibility to resolve issues is shared equally by leaders and members.

Both lay and ordained members find release from past patterns to, now, work together with deeper mutual affirmation and empowerment as the equals they are.

A missionary spirituality for missional members

Each of the baptized senses the Spirit's presence and leading in each of our mission fields. The Spirit leads each of us to find what each of us can do in that mission field to be part of what God is already doing there. Further, as each of us begins to carry out that mission, each finds the Spirit is there helping each of us to do it. Each of us is finding more meaning, more purpose, more direction, and more power for life than any one of us has ever known. For more, see Chapter 10.

A theology that undergirds this book

You will soon notice—if you have not done so already—a theology expressed a number of ways in these pages.

1. God's love and justice have overcome evil, sin, and death in Jesus Christ.
2. Jesus Christ's mission in today's world is to overcome evil, sin, and death with the love and justice of God.

3. Jesus calls us to join his mission and he shares his power, the Holy Spirit of God's love and justice, with us in our life and work with him.
4. We join his mission through baptism and become part of the church where we find the guidance and the power to carry on our daily missions.
5. The Spirit helps us to discern and to live our missions as part of God's mission.

Finally, Chapter 10 draws all of these thoughts and pages together as the spirituality of missional members.

Start early

When you meet newcomers, requesters of baptism, and candidates for confirmation/reaffirmation, recognize that they need to be introduced to the concept of missionary members. Work with them as the missionaries they already are but may not know it. Meet their needs and give yourself practice with "What I am doing right now to make the world a better place" (see Guidepost A on pg. 27 and also Guidepost B on pg. 37, which is the mission discernment form). Both they and you will learn as you go as it should be. Two stories of my own early starts follow.

One early start

I noticed the mission evident in the quality work of an electrician rewiring our home. As he packed up for the day, I asked: "I like the way you work. Can I ask you some questions about your work?"

"Why not?" he answered.

Q: "What keeps you from taking advantage of the home owner who knows little about wiring?"

A: "I want to do it right because, if I don't, there will be complications down the road. I'll have to fix it and, probably, get a bad reputation too. More important, it's the right thing to do. It's the way I was brought up."

Q: "Where did you learn your ethics?"

A: "From my grandmother. She taught me to do right so that when I see the people I work for in the grocery store I can hold my head up."

Q: "Do you see God at work here in any way?"

A: "God will know if no one else does. I am always accountable to God. So is everyone else."

Another early start

Two godparents, a couple, missed the preparation for the baptism of children of their friends. When I reached them for a follow up session, they agreed and added that they wanted their own son, 8, and daughter, 6, baptized. I met with both the parents and their two children on their porch on a summer evening. I explained that baptism was joining our daily missions to Jesus' mission and discussed our daily mission fields. To discern our own missions, all five of us completed four parts of the "What am I doing . . ." form (see Guidepost A, pg. 27) adapted for our use that evening. We worked on the four areas of home, work (school for the children), neighborhood (community), and hungry people (the wider world). We shared our answers with the children going first, and they did so with enthusiasm. I concluded saying that joining the church was joining the people who, in church worship and life, find help on how to live lovingly and fairly and find power to live that way in sharing the bread and the cup. As we parted, the father commented to his wife, "You know what this means. This means we have to start going to church." They did, indeed, become regular worshipers and the mother taught Sunday School and served on the board.

2

Preparing to Lead Missional Members (I)

In This Chapter

Two fundamentals • Your mission fields •
Through "seven mission" eyes • Help for
hearing the missions of others • Samples
of the missions of others • "Part timers"
can do it too

The two fundamentals of missional members

Missional members have two fundamental characteristics. First, the members are the primary missionaries in today's world. Second, a congregation's primary purpose is to support its members in living their daily missions. These two concepts call for a radical reshaping of the life of congregations.

To continue your preparation to be a missional member, start by discerning your own seven mission fields. Use Guidepost A (below) to discern the seven mission fields you are living already. Do it with a colleague or close friend—perhaps a member of your congregation. List what you are doing right now to make the world a better place in seven areas of life. Then, come to see them as seven mission fields.

GUIDEPOST a

What I am doing right now to make the world a more loving and more just place?

Instructions

Jot down what you're doing in each of the following areas to make life better, more loving and more just. Write down big things such as what you do as a volunteer in a hospital, or as an elected public officer, or as a courteous clerk. Also, name even the smallest thing such as always giving up your seat to an elderly person or being the one in your office who circulates birthday cards for others to sign. The key for a small mission is for the activity to be habitual or usual; it's what you try to do all of the time.

1. Home (includes all in my home and close friends)
2. Work (includes home management, school, and volunteer work)
3. Community (my neighborhood, town, or city)
4. Wider world (includes all aspects of the society, culture, economy, government, or environment of the county, state, nation, or world)
5. Leisure (any activity to rest and to refresh myself)
6. Spiritual health (my inner life with God and any activity to meet my own spiritual needs)
7. Church life and outreach (any activity in my church's life and its outreach in service and evangelism and calling others to join Jesus' mission; or in the life of my district, diocese, or communion in the U.S. or worldwide church; or in inter-church or interfaith activities)

What are some of your thoughts after completing this activity? Do you see more clearly how each mission field is unique? Do you have trouble completing some sections such as the wider world or spiritual health? If so, you have probably given to some helping organization or had specific thoughts about the president or political parties, which qualify as wider world. Or you have probably called on God for help in some time of trial, which qualifies as spiritual health. Such moments can suggest how you engage in those mission fields.

Seven missions are too much to focus on every day! Indeed, they are. Actually, one usually lives only one to two missions each day. However, any of the others can arise at any time. Coming home *(a mission)* from a day's work *(a mission)*, a parent hears of a meeting with his daughter's teachers over her poor performance in the eighth grade *(another home mission)*. A Saturday with the family *(a leisure mission)* is claimed by a four-hour planning retreat by her official board *(a church mission)*. An evening planned for buying a new couch *(a home mission)* gives way to an emergency meeting about a problem in the neighborhood *(a community mission)*. Expect to live one or two missions each day while knowing a third may unexpectedly command your time.

Now see and hear the world through your new "seven mission field" eyes

See and hear the missions all around you by looking or listening for a loving or just action or word. When you see or hear one, note it and assign it to its appropriate mission field. For example:

- A programmer tells you how he loves writing programs. He is telling you about a mission at work.
- A mother tells you about her shy ninth grade daughter who has finally overcome her loneliness through her high school swimming team. She is talking about her daughter's mission with home and friends.
- A widower you know teams up with a young mother across the street to host their street's first block party. He is telling you about a community mission.
- A member of your book group says, "Your comments led me to go to my first meeting with the local committee of my political party. She is telling you about her first step into the mission field of wider world.
- A young adult hiker forms a monthly hiking club to learn about trees in the nearby national park. You are hearing how his leisure time has found a mission.

- A new owner of a Sunfish tells you that holding the sheet and tiller in a strong wind is "holding hands with God." She is telling you about living a mission in spiritual health.
- A volunteer Scout leader, a lawyer on his own time, is recruiting churches in a low-income area to sponsor their first troops. He is describing how his recruiting of churches is part of his mission at church.

Are your eyes and ears opening to some of the missions around you? If you are not hearing of or seeing the missions around you, ask others, "What is good about your neighborhood?" or, "What do you like to do in your free time?" Their answer will lie in one of the mission fields. Find similar ways to ask others about life in the other mission fields.

From now on, see and hear of missions from many directions—some examples

Talking with Jessica at a college reunion: "As Doug and I were doing marriage prep with our pastor, he suggested we find a counselor to help us assess issues that might come up in our marriage. We did. After three years and two children, we are still grateful for that advice."

> *Their mission:* building a life and home together.
> *The mission field:* home and friends.

While paging through periodicals: "After a series of threats, hate mail, and hostile phone calls, the Minnesota Chapter of the Council of American-Islamic Relations found a welcoming place at Bethany Lutheran Church in Minneapolis which has a history of supporting advocacy groups and the gay community."[1]

> *Bethany's mission:* making their city inclusive.
> *The mission field:* church life and outreach.

---

[1] *The Christian Century*, March 1, 2017, pp. 8-9

Talking with one of our church's teens: A comment from ninth grader Susan on being part of the Women's March in Washington, January 21, 2017: "There is so much inequality for women; I want to feel as comfortable and valued as men are."

   Her mission: working for equality for women.
   The mission field: the wider world.

More of what helped me to see and hear the missions of others

Don't forget that the church meets the world through its members. My story of acquiring that conviction was advanced by Hendrik Kraemer writing in *A Theology of the Laity* (Westminster, 1958, p. 170): ". . . the real uninterrupted dialog between the Church and world happens through them [the laity]." I met that dialog in the stories of the members of the congregation I served for nineteen years (1956-75). Story telling grew during those years. Helping members to tell their stories was the core of my evangelism work for the national church (1975-93).

   The 1979 *Book of Common Prayer* advanced the vision of missional members when it made three of the promises at Baptism missional promises: proclaiming the Good News of God in Christ; loving your neighbor; and striving for peace and justice and the dignity of everyone. Mark Gibbs, a frequent visitor in my national church office (1976-84), opened me up to the daily mission fields of each member. He compelled my attention because of his long work in helping lay people to connect their faith with all aspects of their life in the world.

   During the late 80s and early 90s, Jim Anderson and I led retirees in conferences to find their "third age missions," as noted above. Jim provided a series of questions for retirees to find their missions. Those questions became the inspiration for the mission discernment forms (see Guidepost B on pg. 37) I developed later. For the first three years of retirement (1994-96), I centered on finding and telling the stories of laity of all ages on mission and sharing their stories in a newsletter. For the first newsletters, I went after the exceptional stories. Then, I began to hear stories of missions of love and justice all around me. I was finding everyone had stories of missions to tell—each person had seven stories when helped to discern them! I told these down-to-earth stories in twelve years of monthly *Member Mission Newsletters*.

That is my story. Let it help you find your own way of seeing that the members in their daily lives are the primary agents of the Gospel in deed and word. They are the primary missionaries. Let it help you to see that you, yourself, are already living seven daily missions.

"Part-timers" can do it too

If you are part-time clergy, here is the story of my part-time work with missional membership. I had two part-time experiences of twenty months each and both in the same church. The second time, I was already deep into missional membership having used various parts of it for twenty years. The first month, I began with briefing the vestry (or official board) on where I was coming from. After a few minutes to introduce missional membership, I proposed a mission statement for discussion and editing so that all of us could own it. The statement we produced continued with minor edits through the next two changes in clergy leadership.

In the next months, I used a missional member framework in every part of my ministry. To baptize infants and young children, I used a missional-member-shaped form of preparation for children who were literate, their parents and godparents.[2]

---

[2] See "Basic Tools 20: Missional Membership Shapes a Baptism and the Preparation for It: Proposal for Baptizing Mary, age 7," click on https://bit.ly/2qdiLXg.

For sermon preparation, I asked eighth-graders through adults for their reflections on living one of the next Sunday's readings, usually the gospel. With the request, I included one or two paragraphs from a commentary interpreting the reading. Their thoughts were included in my sermon and, with their permission, they were cited by name. One of the mission fields was always implied in their reflections and I cited that field when introducing their reflections. Incredibly, I was never refused and continued the practice through the end of my service there.

Pastoral visits with members in their homes, with newcomers, with the sick, with couples preparing for marriage, and with the bereaved for planning funerals were carried on with a mind on the daily missions of the person or people I was with at the time.

If you are an involved church leader or member, the steps outlined in this Chapter will work for you as they have for others – and for me. For me, the seven mission fields shape both my prayers and my daily living. In the current "visioning" process (setting goals for the next five years) of our present church, I will ask questions such as: What is God's mission? Do we want to see baptism as joining God's mission? How will we help members to discern and to live their daily missions? Monthly, I have led reflections on various mission fields using current articles and news stories; we call it "practicing God-talk." The rationale is to provide members with some words or ways to reflect on, talk about, and engage the issues raised by the articles and news stories.

3

Preparing to Lead Missional Members (II)

As a leader you do it first

It's true across all fields of experience. You cannot lead where you will not go yourself. Coaches need to have played the game themselves. As a missional leader, you need to discern and to live your own daily missions.

Read through each of the seven "mission discernment forms" found in Guidepost B below. The eight steps in each field will become the way you think and plan your responses to new situations in any part of life. Print out a set for your own use to write on so that these remain clear.

Following Guidepost B are three additional Guideposts, C, D, and E, that will provide important information about how to complete the mission discernment forms. Guideposts C, D, and E will also be used as part of a four-session Workshop that we will describe in Chapter 4.

It is recommended that you read Guideposts C, D, and E before completing the mission discernment forms.

GUIDEPOST

Mission discernment forms

Home (a current mission or one I will begin)

1. What has God been doing in or saying to me about my life at home (includes all life in the home and life with close friends)? Where are either love or justice or both at work or needed? What message am I getting about it? I will try beginning with: I believe God is . . .

2. As I think about God's message, what is my vision or goal for how I want life to be at home?

3. What am I doing right now to make this vision or goal a reality?

4. What do I still need to do? I will begin with thinking of where I need to bring or to increase caring or love, fairness or justice. I will take into account my skills, talents, gifts, limitations, and convictions.

5. What specifically will I do or continue to do to make my vision or goal a reality, and when will I do it? I will limit myself to just one action. I will have discerned my mission. This is or will be my mission in my home.

6. Who can work with me to carry out this mission? How will I describe the mission to interest him or her? My answer with the person's name and words I might actually use is:

7. When the time is right and with permission, how can I explain how what we are doing is or can be part of God's mission? How will I ask if he or she can agree with my sense of this mission as part of God's mission? My answer with words I might actually use is:

8. When the time is right and with permission, how can I encourage my teammate to turn to the church for help and support? I will begin with how the church helps my life at home and with my friends; that may give me an idea of what to suggest about how it might help him or her. My answer with words I might actually use is:

Work *(a current mission or one I will begin)*

1. What has God been doing in or saying to me about my work (includes home management, school, and volunteer work)? Where are either love or justice or both at work or needed? What message am I getting about it? I will try beginning with: I believe God is . . .

2. As I think about God's message, what is my vision or goal for how I want life to be at work?

3. What am I doing right now to make this vision or goal a reality?

4. What do I still need to do? I will begin with thinking of where I need to bring or to increase caring or love, fairness or justice. I will take into account my skills, talents, gifts, limitations, and convictions.

5. What specifically will I do or continue to do to make my vision or goal a reality and when will I do it? I will limit myself to just one action. I will have discerned my mission. This is or will be my mission in my work.

6. Who can work with me to carry out this mission? How will I describe my mission at work to interest him or her? How will I ask for the other's help? My answer with the person's name and words I might actually use is:

7. When the time is right and with permission, how can I explain how what we are doing is or can be part of God's mission in my work? How will I ask if he or she can agree with my sense of this mission as part of God's mission? My answer with words I might actually use is:

8. When the time is right and with permission, how could I encourage my teammate to turn to the church for help and support? I will begin with how the church helps me in my work; that may give me an idea of what to suggest about how it might help him or her. How will I ask if he or she has ever thought of the church as helping in this way? My answer with words I might actually use is:

Community (*a current mission or one I will begin*)

1. What has God been doing in or saying to me about my community (my neighborhood, town, or city)? Where are

either love or justice or both at work or needed? What message am I getting about it? I will try beginning with: I believe God is . . .

2. As I think about God's message, what is my vision or goal for how I want life to be in my community?

3. What am I doing right now to make this vision or goal a reality?

4. What do I still need to do? I will begin with thinking of where I need to bring or to increase caring or love, fairness or justice. I will take into account my skills, talents, gifts, limitations, and convictions.

5. What specifically will I do or continue to do to make my vision or goal a reality and when will I do it? I will limit myself to just one action. I will have discerned my mission. This is or will be my mission in my community.

6. Who can work with me to carry out this mission? How will I describe the mission to interest him or her? How will I ask for the other's help? My answer with the person's name and words I might actually use is:

7. When the time is right and with permission, how can I explain how what we are doing is or can be part of God's mission? How will I ask if he or she can agree with my sense of this mission as part of God's mission? My answer with words I might actually use is:

8. When the time is right and with permission, how could I encourage my teammate to turn to the church for help and support? I will begin with how the church helps me in my life in my community; that may give me an idea of what to suggest about how it might help him or her. How will I ask if he or she has ever thought of the church as helping in this way? My answer with words I might actually use is:

Wider World *(a current mission or one I will begin)*

1. What has God been doing in or saying to me about the society, culture, economy, government, or environment of the county, state, nation, or world? Where are either love or justice or both at work or needed? What message am I getting? I will try beginning with: I believe God is . . .

2. As I think about God's message, what is my vision or goal for how I want life to be in the wider world?

3. What am I doing right now to make this vision or goal a reality?

4. What do I still need to do? I will begin with thinking of where I need to bring or to increase caring or love, fairness or justice. I will take into account my skills, talents, gifts, limitations, and convictions.

5. What, specifically, will I do or continue to do to make my vision or goal a reality and when will I do it? I will limit myself to just one action. This is or will be my mission in the wider world.

6. Who can work with me to carry out this mission? How will I describe the mission to interest him or her? How will I ask for the other's help? My answer with the person's name and words I might actually use is:

7. When the time is right and with permission, how can I explain how what we are doing is or can be part of God's mission? How will I ask if he or she can agree with my sense of this mission as part of God's mission? My answer with words I might actually use is:

8. When the time is right and with permission, how could I encourage my teammate to turn to the church for help and support? I will begin with how the church helps me in my life in the wider world; that may give me an idea of what to suggest about how it might help him or her. How will I ask if he or she has ever thought of the church as helping in this way? My answer with words I might actually use is:

Leisure *(a current mission or one I will begin)*

1. What has God been doing in or saying to me about my leisure (includes any activity that rests or refreshes me)? Where are either love or justice or both at work or needed? What message am I getting about it? I will try beginning with: I believe God is . . .

2. As I think about God's message, what is my vision or goal for how I want life to be in my leisure time?

3. What am I doing right now to make this vision or goal a reality?

4. What do I still need to do? I will begin with thinking of where I need to bring or to increase caring or love, fairness or justice. I will take into account my skills, talents, gifts, limitations, and convictions.

5. What specifically will I do or continue to do to make my vision or goal a reality and when will I do it? I will limit myself to just one action. I will have discerned my mission. This is or will be my mission in my leisure.

6. Who can work with me to carry out this mission? How will I describe the mission to interest him or her? How will I ask for the other's help? My answer with the person's name and words I might actually use is:

7. When the time is right and with permission, how can I explain how what we are doing is or can be part of God's mission? How will I ask if he or she can agree with my sense of this mission as part of God's mission? My answer with words I might actually use is:

8. When the time is right and with permission, how could I encourage my teammate to turn to the church for help and support? I will begin with how the church helps me in my pursuit of leisure; that may give me an idea of what to suggest about how it might help him or her. How will I ask if he or she has ever thought of the church as helping in this way? My answer with words I might actually use is:

Spiritual health
(a current mission or one I will begin)

1. What has God been doing in or saying to me about my spiritual health (my inner life with God and any activity to meet my spiritual needs)? Where are either love or justice or both at work or needed? What message am I getting about it? I will try beginning with: I believe God is . . .

2. As I think about God's message, what is my vision or goal for what I want for my spiritual health?

3. What am I doing right now to make this vision or goal a reality?

4. What do I still need to do? I will begin with thinking of where I need to bring or to increase caring or love, fairness or justice. I will take into account my skills, talents, gifts, limitations, and convictions.

5. What specifically will I do or continue to do to make my vision or goal a reality and when will I do it? I will limit myself to just one action. I will have discerned my mission. This is or will be my mission for my spiritual health.

6. Who can work with me to carry out this mission? How will I describe the mission to interest him or her? How will I ask for the other's help? My answer with the person's name and words I might actually use is:

7. When the time is right and with permission, how can I explain how what we are doing is or can be part of God's

mission? How will I ask if he or she can agree with my sense of this mission as part of God's mission? My answer with words I might actually use is:

8. When the time is right and with permission, how could I encourage my teammate to turn to the church for help and support? I will begin with how the church helps me in my spiritual life; that may give me an idea of what to suggest about how it might help him or her. How will I ask if he or she has ever thought of the church as helping in this way? My answer with words I might actually use is:

Church life and outreach
(a current mission or one I will begin)

1. What has God been doing in or saying to me about my church's life and its outreach in service and evangelism and calling others to join Jesus' mission; or in the life of my district, diocese, or communion in the United States; or worldwide church; or in interchurch or interfaith activities? Where are either love or justice or both at work or needed? What message am I getting about it? I will try beginning with: I believe God is . . .

2. As I think about God's message, what is my vision or goal for how I want to participate in my church's life and outreach?

3. What am I doing right now to make this vision or goal a reality?

4. What do I still need to do? I will begin with thinking of where I need to bring or to increase caring or love, fairness or justice. I will take into account my skills, talents, gifts, limitations, and convictions.

5. What specifically will I do or continue to do to make my vision or goal a reality and when will I do it? I limit myself to just one action. I will have discerned my mission. This is or will be my mission in my church's life and outreach.

6. Who can work with me to carry out this mission? How will I describe the mission to interest him or her? How will I ask for the other's help? My answer with the person's name and words I might actually use is:

7. When the time is right and with permission, how can I explain how what we are doing is or can be part of God's mission? How will I ask if he or she can agree with my sense of this mission as part of God's mission? My answer with words I might actually use is:

8. When the time is right and with permission, how could I encourage my teammate to turn to the church for help and support? I will begin with how the church helps me in my life at church; that may give me an idea of what to suggest about how it might help him or her. How will I ask if he or she has ever thought of the church as helping in this way? My answer with words I might actually use is:

GUIDEPOST C

The pattern of the mission discernment forms and notes for completing them

First, a word about "discernment" in the title. Webster's defines it in a charming way, "to detect with the eyes a figure approaching through the fog."[1] Discerning what God wants is never a fully error-free perception. Test what you discern. Do you sense love or justice present or needed? Does what you sense accord with biblical insights into how God works? Does it accord with your own experience? You might pray "God approve what I discern where it is right and correct what I discern where it is wrong." Avoid claiming absolute accuracy for what you discern.

The forms all the follow the same pattern for each mission field. The form for Home will be our sample. The key questions to note are in bold. The first question is foundational for the rest of the questions. It asks, in what way is God already at work in this area of your life? It reads:

1. What has God been doing in or saying to me about my life at home (includes all life in the home and with close friends)? What message am I getting about it? I will try beginning with: I believe God is . . .

Are you clear and specific in your answer? Do you actually mention God? A clue for sensing what God is doing is looking for wherever you see love or justice at work, the distinctive signs of God's Spirit at work. Another clue is the opposite; where are love or justice needed. God is already at

---

[1] Merriam-Webster's Collegiate Dictionary, Eleventh Edition, 2003.

work, somehow, to bring love and justice wherever they are needed.

You may see or sense a sign of God, the Holy Spirit, already working to bring or to increase love or justice there. By the way, the Holy Spirit is often understood as God at work in people and in the world around us. That is how it is used in this book.

This first question keeps you focused on discerning what God wants. Seek to connect what you will do with what you sense God is already doing. Beware of starting with what you want or need because you will probably end up telling God what you will do rather than discerning how you will join what God is already doing in that part of your life.

Questions 2, 3, and 4 help you to discern various options for ways to join what God is already doing.

2. As I think about God's message, what is my vision or goal for how I want life to be at home?
3. What am I doing right now to make this vision or goal a reality?
4. What do I still need to do? Begin with thinking of where I need to bring or to increase caring or love, fairness or justice; and of how I can do it working with my skills, talents, gifts, limitations, and convictions.

Do your answers lead up to Question 5?
In Question 5, you choose how you will actually join what you sense God is already doing; and when you will do it.

5. What specifically will I do or continue to do to make my vision or goal a reality, and when will I do it?

Limit yourself to just one action and be clear and specific? Do you say when you will do it? This is or will be your mission in your home and with your friends. We have tended to call loving and just actions in our Monday to Saturday living "good deeds." They are really missions. Also, note the parenthesis that follows the name of each mission field, "(a current mission or one I will begin)." The mission you choose may well be a mission you are already living, such as being a responsible parent, a competent worker, or an engaged citizen.

Questions 6, 7, and 8 help you to find and work with a teammate who can help you to reflect on your words and actions and to plan your next steps.

6. Who can work with me to carry out this mission? How will I describe the mission to interest him or her? My answer with the person's name and words I might actually use is:

Do you name a specific person and is your description of the mission inviting?

7. When the time is right and with permission, how can I explain that what we are doing is or can be part of God's mission? How will I ask if he or she can agree with my sense of this mission as part of God's mission? My answer with words I might actually use is:

Is your explanation clear? Does it refer explicitly to God or to God's mission? How will you ask if your teammate agrees this is or can be part of God's mission?

8. When the time is right and with permission, how can I encourage my teammate to turn to the church for help and support? I will begin with how the church helps me; that may give me an idea of what to suggest for how it might help him or her. My answer with words I might actually use is:

Is your description of how the church helps you clear and specific? Is your description of how the church might help your teammate clear and specific?

GUIDEPOST

Working with the first two questions of the mission discernment form

You and the Spirit as you start

As you work with these forms, remember God's Spirit is with you to help you make life more loving and more just in each area of life.[1] You may want to pray for God's help.

> Lord, may your Spirit help me to see my life and life around me as it is.

As you work, remember the signs of the Spirit's work and presence are love and justice. Where you meet love or justice, the Spirit is at work. God is there somewhere, in someone, in some force working to bring what seems to be missing or to strengthen what looks weak.

Remember too, the Spirit is at work in the familiar or commonplace. The Spirit accepts and works with you wherever you are and in whatever you do. God, the Spirit, values small as well as large works. It's the presence of love and justice in whatever you do that counts. Your work in each mission field opens the possibility for God to make maximum use of your unique combination of experiences, insights, and talents. The Spirit will put them to good use and help you to shore up any weaknesses.

---

[1] For a fuller understanding of you and the Spirit see Chapter 10.

The first two questions
and a missionary spirituality

The first question asks "What has God been doing in or say-ing to me about . . . (my life in a mission field)?" To sense what God is doing or saying in your life is not as "other-worldly" as it sounds. The second question asks ". . . what is my vision or goal for how I want life to be . . . (in a mission field)?" The answers are yours to discover.

Begin with recalling your most pressing concern or one of many pressing concerns. Pressing concerns come from ar-eas of life like these. What is going well for you? What keeps coming to your mind? What concerns you the most? What needs correction in your life? What are others most con-cerned about? What is unfair or unjust in the world around you that needs correction? Once you have chosen the concern to work on, select the mission field in which it falls.

Now, find what God is doing or saying in this mission field.

- Among your current experiences in this field, select the most important or one of the most important experi-ences.
- Recall as many of the specific details of the experience (people involved, what was done, what was said, where, when, etc.) as you can.
- Then, ask where in this experience do you find love or justice to be present or needed. Where love or justice are present, God is doing or saying something through that love or justice. Where love or justice are absent or weak, God is present doing or saying something to bring or to increase them. What you perceive God to be doing or saying is your answer to the first question.

Next, choose your vision or goal for life in this mission field.

- Mindful of what God is doing or saying in this field, what are some of the things you want to see happen that would make life there more loving or more just?

- Among the possible things you want to see happen, which is the one you want most to see happen. That is your goal or vision for what you want life to be like in that field or part of your life.
- Now you are ready to move on to the rest of the questions on the mission discernment form.

We will now look at a story about someone we will call Gil that exemplifies a way to practice moving from what is happening in a mission field to what God is doing or saying there and your vision or goal of what you want life in that field to be like.

Gil manages the production section of his company. He admires the way his company respects its employees. When someone's illness is using up allotted sick time, the company finds ways to help. In a recent economic downturn, company layoffs were kept to a minimum.

As I reflected on his story, I imagined what Gil would understand God to be doing or saying to him about a goal for his work. I came up with Gil believing God was saying that he should respect the people he supervises. Gil's goal might be to be fair and considerate in leading his section.

Seven stories with blanks for you to imagine how the participants might have answered the first two questions.

1. Alan and Raquel at home

Alan is a state trooper and Raquel works part-time in checkout at a grocery store in order to have time to be at home with their four-year-old son. Alan thanks God each day when he gets home safely. He believes he gets help to keep to his principles to be fair and to treat people as he wants to be treated. Raquel manages to just barely pay the bills each month. Both parents are in good health. Both of them thank God for their life and home.

Raquel might write: "I believe God is helping us to come up with the money we need to pay our bills." For her goal now, she might write: "This month I will write down everything we pay for and see what I learn about having enough at the end of the month."

Alan might write: "I believe God is helping us to take the time we need to make our marriage and home work."

For his goal, he might write: "My goal for now is to keep all three of us safe and healthy."

2. Audrey at work

With her youngest in the ninth grade, Audrey becomes a trainer for a national organization that alerts pre-teens and teens to the dangers of smoking. With unusual success, she teaches high school seniors to present the case against smoking to pre-teens as well as teens. News of her success spreads across her organization.

She might write: "I believe God is helping me to grow in skill for working with youth."

As a goal forms, she might write: "I want to try to train my colleagues to train young people."

3. Len in his community

Len, a retired Episcopal priest in a Southeastern state, is appointed by the court to work with the social services of his state. He is assigned to neglected or abused children and youth as a mentor who will visit them at least once a month.

First, Len visits their schools for information about these youth as part of being able to see that they get a "fair shake." When interviewed, he was working with a girl, seven, who was mentally handicapped, and a boy, seventeen, who was reading at the third-grade level. He finds the work satisfying and enjoyable.

He might write: "I believe God is using me to help these youth to feel better about themselves."

He might write as an emerging goal: "I want to interest more retired clergy of all faiths in this work."

4. *Janet in the wider world*

Janet's carpool of teachers was complaining about the likelihood of higher taxes if universal health care was enacted by the new administration. Janet, a single mother of two, decided it was a time to speak up. "I'd pay more in taxes. I make a good income and have good health coverage. I can't imagine what life would be like for a single mother on less income with no health insurance." After a period of silence, there were no more complaints about taxes.

Janet might write: "I believe God is letting me know I should continue to speak up on social issues."

Reflecting further, she might write: "I want to continue speaking up when I hear views on social issues that miss some crucial truths."

5. *Michelle in her leisure*

Michelle's fiancé did so well in his work for an airline that both can fly free to ski in European resorts. To her surprise, Michelle finds she is not only a quick learner but has a gift for skiing.

She might write: "I believe God wants me to develop my gift for skiing as part of our life together."

As a vision takes shape, she might write: "Wherever we ski, I will take some time for a lesson or two to increase my skill and enjoyment of our time together."

6. *Will and spiritual health*

Will, a bishop, had an idea for Christmas night. With only the lights of the tree, he asked each member of his family, his wife, his son of 14, his daughter of 10, and himself, to share "a time or experience when God, Jesus, or the Holy Spirit touched your mind or heart in a real way—a way that helped you to grow in faith and life." He learned things about each one that he had not known before.

He might write: "I believe God is leading me to new ways to share our faith together as a family."

He sees a goal forming and might write: "I will look for both religious and secular holidays when we can do this sharing of faith and life."

7. Harry in the church and its outreach

Harry, a forester for the U.S. government, has just guided a group in his small church (Sunday attendance averages 15-20 parishioners) through the mission discernment forms. He makes sure the relevant details of each answer are included and that they are specific. Harry finds that completing the forms helps them to a sense of God's call coming to them wherever they are. Next, the group will read and discuss Thomas Merton's *Bridges to Contemplative Living*. At the end of each week, each shares "How will I live this week on the basis of what we have studied?" Each will pray for the week the prayer of the person on the right; and, next week, each will share experiences in the area of the prayer he or she asked for.

Harry might write: "I believe God is leading me to keep this kind of group going in our church."

A goal may be forming to lead him to write: "To sharpen my ability to guide them, I will rotate my daily prayers among the seven mission fields, note each day's prayer; and reflect on life in that area the next day."

GUIDEPOST

A guide for completing a mission discernment form

Question 1

1. What has God been doing in or telling me about (this mission field)? What message am I getting about it? I will try beginning with: I believe God is . . .

   Is God mentioned? Avoid a wholly secular answer. Is your response clear? Clarity is more important than theological accuracy.

Questions 2, 3, and 4

2. As I think about God's message, what is my vision or goal for how I want life to be (in/at this mission field)?

3. What am I doing right now to make this vision or goal a reality?

4. What do I still need to do? Begin with thinking of where bring or to increase caring or love, fairness or justice; and doing it with my skills, talents, gifts, limitations, and convictions.

   Do your responses lead up to question 5?

Question 5

5. What specifically will I do or continue to do to make my vision or goal a reality, and when will I do it? I will limit

myself to just one action. This is or will be my mission in (this mission field).

*The key question: does it state a **specific word or action** and **when** it will be done?*

Question 6

6. Who can work with me to carry out this mission? How will I describe the mission to interest him or her? An answer with the person's name and words I might actually use:

*Do you name a **specific person**? Does your description of the mission sound **inviting**?*

Question 7

7. When the time is right and with permission, how can I explain how what we are doing is or can be part of God's mission? My answer with words I might actually use:

*Is the explanation **clear**? Do you **make explicit reference** to God, God's mission, your faith, the Bible, or the church?*

Question 8

8. When the time is right and with permission, how can I encourage my teammate to turn to the church for help and support? I will begin with how the church helps me; that may give me an idea of what to suggest for how it might help him or her. My answer with words I might actually use:

*Is your description of how the church helps you and how it might help the other **clear and specific**?*

Note how essential questions 7 and 8 are to the fullness of your mission. A mission should have these two parts – what we do and what we say about God and the church. The word without the deed is empty; the deed without the word is dark.

More about a teammate and questions 6,7, and 8

Try to have a teammate for each mission. The going two-by-two pattern of the New Testament (Mark 6:7) is good for missional members, too.

- If what you share is already familiar to your teammate, your sharing is a useful affirming of the power available to us in church life.
- If your teammate is not a churchgoer, hearing how the church helps you can open the door to a dimension of church life and mission that may be new for him or her.
- Still further, if your teammate is not a church member, a mission is still incomplete until we encourage him or her to explore Jesus' people and his mission.

Regarding Question 6, look for a person who can test the reality of your plans and goals, who will offer ideas, and who, during the mission, will listen and comment on what did not work as well as what did work. Your teammate does not have to be a church member but does need to have love and justice as primary values and a good share of wisdom about people. With love and justice among the primary values of your potential teammate, he or she is already part of God's mission without seeing it that way.

Regarding Question 7, draw on your knowledge of the potential teammate to describe the mission in a way that will be easy to understand and will be inviting as well challenging. Regarding Question 8, like you yourself, your teammate will want ideas of where to go for help.

Questions 7 and 8 are much of what we know as evangelism – telling of God's presence and work among us and asking for your potential teammate's comment on this view of life. This approach puts evangelism inside of mission where it should have been all along. Your sharing is more easily grasped when offered in the midst of a loving or just mission. The sharing will take less time than telling your story and may be heard much more deeply. If your teammate is not a churchgoer, hearing how the church helps you can open the door to a dimension of church life that may be new to him or to her. If what you share is already familiar to your potential teammate, your sharing is still a useful affirming of the power available to us in church life.

End of Guidepost E
Now, complete the mission discernment of
your choice (see Guidepost B on pg. 37).

Closing Thoughts

Finding the skills, talents, and gifts needed to fulfill your missions

You already have many of the skills, talents, and gifts you will need to fulfill each specific mission. You and the Spirit have been developing them over the years. They are implied in the mission discernment form you have just completed. Read through your completed form asking yourself "What skill, talent, or gift is implied in each answer?" You may find more than one skill, talent, or gift implied in one answer. List all that come to mind on a note pad.

For the best results, ask a friend to help you. As you read each answer, your friend names the skill, talent, or gift implied in each answer and lists them on a note pad. You may hear skills, talents, and gifts you have not recognized in yourself. Further, expect some skill, talent, or gift to be named that you will need but do not have at the moment. Pray for the Spirit's help. You will probably find you are able to develop and to do the "new thing" needed – another joint work of your own and of the Spirit working with you (read more about this in Chapter 10: The spirituality of missional members).

Notice too that you, or your friend, have used today's words without using the biblical names for gifts as found in

Romans 12:6-8, 1 Corinthians 12:8-10, or Ephesians 4:11-12. Those three lists from Paul are in a first century framework of church life. You are in the 21st century and use today's words to talk about today's skills, talents, and gifts.[1]

---

[1] See Guidepost I (pg. 96) for more about skills, talents, and gifts in contemporary language.

4

Leading your board into Session 1
of the first board workshop,
*Understanding and Growing as
Missional Members*

This chapter has two parts; the first part guides the leader of the workshop; and the second part is the first session of the workshop. Find in part one: the changes the workshop makes; its purpose and goals for you; its long-term outcomes; what each session does; what to expect; your own goals; and more for you as the workshop's leader.

The second part: purpose and goals of the workshop for its participants; some anticipated outcomes; getting a feel for the seven mission fields; the need to center on love and justice; and five marks of a mission. The workshop: its purpose; likely outcomes; seven areas of daily life as mission fields; centering on love and justice; and five marks of a mission.

The next – and big – step and why take it

You probably sense that to make supporting the daily missions of each member the basic purpose of your church is a radical change. It changes everything. Compare and contrast these changes in mission as it is lived in many churches and in the missional church.

In many churches, the sacred and the secular, the church and the world, are not only seen to be very different but, at times, in conflict;

> whereas in the missional church, the place of the sacred is with the secular to make life in the world more loving and more just.

In many churches, both leaders and members have only a limited understanding that they are already living the mission in their daily lives;

> whereas in the missional church, both leaders and members fully understand the call to live the mission in their daily lives and are deepening their living of their missions day by day.

In many churches, the members live the mission within the church and its programs and see what they do outside the church as secondary;

> whereas in the missional church, the members seek to live the mission at any time in any one of seven mission fields (home, work, community, the wider world, leisure, spiritual health, and church life and outreach) as the circumstances require.

In many churches, only the mission field of church life and outreach is primary;

> whereas in the missional church, all seven mission fields are of equal importance.

In many churches, members can easily ignore fields of mission which they may find burdensome such as social issues or spiritual health or community;

> whereas in the missional church, members are challenged to examine their life in all seven of the mission fields and find their mission in each one.

In many churches, members can easily wrangle with each other over petty issues of budget, control, and rank:

> whereas in the missional church all members are on the same "street" and face the same basic issues of being loving and just wherever they are.

In many churches, newcomers considering membership are briefed on all the good things the church offers and the strengths of the communion it belongs to;

> whereas in the missional church, newcomers learn that when they join the church they are joining God's mission to make the world more loving and just with God's help and that they will learn to live that mission in all seven areas of life.

In many churches, newcomers are welcomed and guided into church related activities (usually in just one mission field) while activities outside the church are seldom mentioned if not overlooked altogether;

> whereas in the missional church, newcomers are quickly guided into all seven mission fields as places for their concern and of their responsibility.

In many churches, leaders and members celebrate primarily the accomplishments of the members within the church and its programs;

> whereas in the missional church, leaders and members celebrate the accomplishments of the members in any of the seven mission fields.

Taken together, these and other changes made by missional member churches add up to a radical change of everything. Radical change does not come overnight. Radical change comes slowly. The first year, your own teaching and preaching will change. Members will rejoice to hear that their loving and just words and deeds of every day are part of God's mission—signs of the Holy Spirit helping them every moment.

More and more they will ask for and tell each other about loving and just moments in daily life in the brief moments of small talk before meetings and during coffee hour after worship. In five years, signs of radical change will appear frequently as members and non-members alike know that joining this church is joining God's mission of caring and fairness.

So, take heart. The members are much further along in living their daily missions than you may think. In fact, they are already on their way more than they may even realize. They may already be: responsible parents, a home mission; competent employees, a work mission; and engaged citizens, a wider world mission. Your role as leader is to increase their awareness of: what they are already doing that is missional; what will help them to grow in missional living; and what will help them to sense God's presence and help in every moment.

Leading your board and holding your first workshop

It is now time to lead your board to implement supporting the members in living their daily missions as the purpose of the congregation. Your board will consist of at least 7 members of your church who you believe will be capable of helping to lead others in missional membership. Ideally, the board will meet monthly.

To introduce your board to missional membership, propose a workshop of four weekly sessions held in the evenings for two to two-and-half hours each; end it at the next board meeting. Share with them a copy of your purpose and goals for the workshop, the basic activities and insights of each session, and where you believe they will be by the end of the workshop; all of which are outlined below. Simply print out the next paragraphs through ". . . becomes their workshop as well."

Refer to Guidepost F below and review the purpose and goals for the workshop, as well as some anticipated outcomes.

GUIDEPOST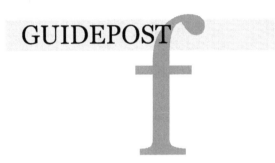

Our purpose and goals for the workshop; and some anticipated outcomes

Purpose: To explore being missional members and to outline next steps to continue in this direction.

Goals:

(1) To introduce the board to becoming missional members.
(2) To understand that God's mission includes making every part of life more loving and more just with God's help.
(3) To define a missional member as a member who knows and seeks to live God's mission in every part of daily life.
(4) To develop (or redevelop) a mission statement for our church.
(5) To list and to commit ourselves to ways that enable all members to become missional members.

Some anticipated outcomes of what missional members will do

For the congregation

Missional members go into the world to live out their missions wherever they are. Their example leads all of the members to seek to do the same. The congregation rejoices to see growing fulfillment of the promises of baptism in daily life.

For the members

Missional members affirm that everything members do to make the world more loving and more just is known and valued by God. Everything from preparing food and doing the dishes to being leaders in Congress is recognized and treasured by God. Members are recognized for already living lovingly and justly as full partners in God's mission.

For the world

All who, in various ways, are working for a more loving and just world will be strengthened by the missional members who add their will and energy to the various works under way or who will lead others into new works for a better world.

Each session will illustrate and practice these basic activities and insights:

Session One: describing missional members and the seven mission fields of each member.

Session Two: meeting mission discernment forms, understanding them, and choosing the form for a mission field of your choice.

Session Three: finding help for your mission, changing from forming church members to forming missional members; drafting a mission statement for your congregation and considering first steps in using it; and beginning a plan to practice living the mission discerned in Session 2.

Session Four: each participant shares his or her experience and learnings from living the mission discerned in Session 2; and the board starts to plan specific ways to implement the first steps in living the congregation's mission statement. This session is an official meeting of the board.

By the end of fourth session, the board will:

- have a fairly comprehensive overview of building a congregation of missional members that can be viewed by anyone;
- have a working introduction to using mission discernment forms because they will have completed a form of their own choice, have practiced it, and have shared their experiences, observations, and learnings with two other members; and
- have a sense of what living as missional members can do for them individually, for every church member, and for a more loving and just world.

Share with the board your goals

While these are huge goals and expectations, you believe they can grasp and seek to grow in living them day by day. Your goal is to help them to continue the path they already follow and improve it as appropriate. For now, take a few minutes for individual reflection; then, ask for their questions, comments, or suggestions. With their questions, comments or suggestions in mind, edit the proposed purpose and goals of the workshop as needed so that it becomes their workshop as well.

More about the workshop for you as leader

The workshop offered here has four sessions of about two and never more than two and a half hours. The various sub-parts of the sessions are described below in sections, each with its own number.

The workshop uses procedures I have used often. You know your board so adapt the details of the workshop to your situation. The choice of which sections to use is up to you. Select from the wealth of background material in each section what is needed by your particular participants. The actual time to allow for each section is also your choice.

Each weekly session should begin with gathering and praying, and end with reflection and closing. As for which additional sections to choose for each session of the workshop, I have found the following sections to be fairly essential:

Session 1
- clarifying our purpose (Section 2);
- seven mission fields (Sections 3 and 4);
- love and justice as reliable guides (Section 5);
- five marks of a mission (Section 6);

Session 2
- getting acquainted with mission discernment forms (Section 10);
- the pattern of these forms (Section 11);
- working with the first two questions of the mission discernment form (Section 12)—use this section if sensing God's work in one's life and naming a vision or goal based on what is sensed is difficult for the participants;
- each completes a mission discernment form (Section 13);

Session 3
- discerning your skills, talents, and gifts for one of your missions (Section 17);
- how church members can become missional members (Section 18);
- drafting a mission statement for the congregation (Section 19);

- planning for living, and reflecting on a mission (Section 21)

Session 4
- sharing experiences and learnings from living a mission (Section 24);
- next steps with the mission statement (Section 25); and
- reflecting on the four sessions of the workshop (Section 26).

The length of each section is only an estimate. Each section's length is your decision. The sections make up each session, which should run 2 to 2½ hours.

<u>Some more specific suggestions and comments</u> for you as the workshop leader.

- Some of the directions are for you, some are for you to give to the whole group. "(Suggest)" will indicate directions for the whole group. Beyond that, many times the context tells which is which.
- Include in your proposal for the workshop a schedule for the four sessions that allows a week between Sessions 1, 2, and 3 for reflection and integration of the last session's learnings. Provide two to three weeks or so between Sessions 3 and 4 to be sure each has time for doing his or her mission in preparation for Session 4.
- Where possible, a week between the sessions allows time for reflection and integration of the last session's leanings.
- Give out the plan for the full session as each session begins. You will save time and, more importantly, leave the full material for each person to consult for reference at any time.
- A "guidepost" is a page or more of ideas and activities that explain the section in which it appears. Some

leaders have found them the core of the workshop. Several guideposts have *background as needed* – namely, biblical or historical support for the views presented in the guideposts. Two factors, the participants' questions and available time, will guide your choice of what background is needed by your board.

- Begin each section with its title, its purpose, and your estimate of how many minutes will be needed to complete it.
- The time noted for each session is only an estimate. Aim for sessions of about 120 minutes (two hours) and not more than 160 minutes (two and a half hours); a sensible goal is 135 minutes (two and a quarter hours) for each session. Give the members the time you believe they will actually need when estimating the length of sessions.
- Sessions should be focused on learning by doing and time for discussion.
- Prepare the white board or easel pad postings for an evening session well before the evening begins; also plan when and how to display each one before the session begins.
- As much as possible, you, as leader, do what you ask the group to do. For example, you also complete Guidepost A in Session 1. However, do not pair up to share your choice of mission as in Section 11 of Session 2. The context usually suggests which to do. This practice increases your empathy for the participants.

This workshop is a rich opportunity to develop leadership potential in your board. The activities in the workshop encourage the leadership qualities of talking easily with others, listening in depth, learning to work with new teaching methods, planning and using time with care, and longing to see the church make a difference in today's world.

In brief, the workshop is part of this book as a way to help you as a leader to understand more clearly the elements necessary for missional members to become the norm for your church. The plan for the workshop follows. The leader is assumed to be you or you and a co-leader. Read what follows not as commands but as directions you will modify to fit your situation.

Session 1
of the Workshop

*Understanding and Growing
as Missional Members*

(Section 1) Gathering and praying

About 5 minutes
Purpose: Gather and greet one another; and pray for the Spirit's presence.

Greet one another. To build community, ask board members to partner with someone they know less well. Be seated. Pray for the Spirit: to lead and to teach us today; to guide the congregation we serve; and for us, with God's help, to be part of God's ongoing work to make all of life more loving and more just.

(Section 2) Clarifying our purpose
About 12-15 minutes
Purpose: to clarify our purpose and goals and to begin to explore developing missional members.

Pass out Guidepost F

Participants read Guidepost F aloud. Go on to share briefly what excites you about missional members; what it has done for you; what it might do for the congregation; and what it might do for the world. Comment that with God's help, you hope to lead them step by step into the missional member vision and what it is like to live it day by day.

For 3-4 minutes, each pair discusses: is the purpose clear; which goal needs clarification; and what goals might be added. Also discuss the value of the anticipated outcomes of what missional members will do.

Ask for comments, needed clarifications, and additions to the purpose and goals. Modify the purpose and goals as appropriate.

(Section 3) Seven areas of daily life

About 25-30 minutes
Purpose: to get a "feel" for the seven different areas of daily life.

Pass out Guidepost A

Participants read Guidepost A aloud. Emphasize that they should enter whatever comes to mind whether large or small. Advise keeping to what is loving or just as the guide for what to enter. Allow about 5-6 minutes to complete the form.

Next, go around the group sharing what each has entered. Begin with yourself to encourage sharing. If someone cannot complete one of the fields, ask the others to help. Others may know the person well enough to name actions or words the sharer has not thought of. Keen guesses from others may also be on target. All will value gaining greater knowledge of one another.

When all have shared, outline briefly the source of the seven areas. Martin Luther wrote specifically about home, work, the community, and the church. Today's world calls for adding the wider world (from social norms to systems); adding leisure; and adding spiritual health.

You may want to share that accounts of life in these seven fields abound in both the Hebrew and Christian Bibles.

Two examples: Ruth promises that wherever Naomi goes will be her home too (Ruth 1:16-17). Exploitation of the poor leads Micah to address the wider world by calling all of Israel to "do justice and to love mercy" (Micah 6:8). Later in the workshop, we will practice a way for each of us to explore each of the seven areas of our own lives.

Ask and discuss how ready are they to use this sense of seven different areas of daily life.

(Section 4) These seven areas are our daily mission fields

About 10-12 minutes
Purpose: to see these seven areas as mission fields.
Post on an easel or white board the following:

home: includes all in the home and close friends
work: includes home management, school, and volunteer work

community: neighborhood, town, or city
wider world: all arenas of the county, state, or nation

leisure: all that rests and refreshes
spiritual health: one's inner life with God and meeting one's spiritual needs

church life and outreach: any activity, local to world wide

Directing attention to this list, comment that these seven areas of daily life are our daily mission fields. God is on mission in each one of them. We discern what God is doing there and choose how we will join what God is already doing there. That becomes our mission in that field. While at any given moment each of us has seven missions, we do not carry on all seven every day. Usually, each of us carries on one to three missions in a given day. Missions at home and at work often take up five days of each week. A third mission, such as community or wider world, may join these two during the week. Weekends often center on leisure, spiritual health, and church.

Invite questions or comments.

Ask for and discuss the group's comfort level with the word "mission." You may discover that "mission" is a bad word for some. They remember stories of how missionaries have abused the people to whom they were sent and their culture. If so, post where all can see two columns. Head the left column "Abusive missions" and head the right column "Loving and just missions." Brainstorm a list for the column on the left and, then, for the one on the right. Draw an "X" over the list on the left and affirm the list on the right as suggesting the way we seek to practice mission day by day.

Even if "mission" is not a bad word for the participants, it may be a bad word for others. Adapting this approach may help others to value the words and actions of mission. If any are still uneasy with the word, ask them to be "watchdogs" alerting the rest to possible abuses when they arise.

(Section 5) Our centering on love and justice are rooted in the biblical accounts of God's words and works

Purpose: to see love and justice as ever present and reliable guides to find God's presence and work and, therefore, to find God on mission and to find our own missions.

Pass out Guidepost G.

GUIDEPOST

Love and justice: God's mission and our missions

Love and justice are ever present and reliable guides to find God on mission and to find our missions. Wherever we meet love and justice, we are meeting God at work among us. Wherever love and justice are missing, God is at work somewhere to bring them. If we do not see where God is at work now, we will see it in time.

Love and justice have guided the biblical writers from the first. Their stories are our guides to find God at work and they guide us to find our own missions as well. Both testaments abound in love and justice.

God's love guides the Israelites in their escape from Pharaoh (Exodus 15:13) and Hosea hears God say his love cannot give up on a rebellious people (Hosea 11:8). Matthew, Mark, and Luke record Jesus' teaching that loving God and loving your neighbor as yourself are the foundation of the law and the prophets (Matthew 22:37-40, Mark 12:29-31, Luke 10:27-28, 8-34). Enemies are to be loved as well (Matthew 5:44).

Micah's call "to do justice" (Micah 6:8) in the midst of oppression of the poor and Isaiah's vision of a just society (Isaiah 65:20-23) proclaim God's justice. In Isaiah's vision, children do not die, old people live in dignity, people live in the houses they build, and farmers eat what they plant. Jesus challenged the injustice of Jewish laws that called for the faithful to avoid eating with tax collectors who served the foreign power of Rome and sinners who had fallen into ways harmful to themselves and to others. Matthew sees Jesus as fulfilling Isaiah's prophecy of one who "brings justice to victory" (Matthew 12:20). Finally, Jesus' resurrection overcomes the injustice of his crucifixion (Acts 2:23-24 and Romans 1:4). We, too, are raised with him to new life (Ephesians 2:4-6).

To the participants

Today, we use love and justice in many ways. This book works from a contemporary description of love and justice that can help you to discern signs of God's mission in your life and in today's world. They can also help you to discern your own daily missions as part of God's mission.

- Love is seeking without limit, to value others as they really are, to care for them, to forgive their faults, and to help them to put their skills and talents to their best possible use.
- Justice is the "public" face of love. In public life, we love by seeking for everyone equal access to food, housing, just wages, health care, education and whatever else helps them to become all that they are created to be and to put their skills and talents to their best possible use.

A different reader reads each of the five paragraphs in Guidepost G.

In pairs, each shares a favorite biblical verse or story of love and a favorite biblical verse or story of justice and what gives each verse or story its special appeal.

After a few minutes, ask for three examples of love and three of justice. Then, invite a few comments, suggestions, or criticisms of any kind.

(Section 6) Five marks of a mission

About 20 minutes
Purpose: to explore five marks of a mission.

Post the five marks of mission from Guidepost H so that all can see them as you describe each one. "Each mission has five marks," and ask five people to read them. Perhaps, at the third, "missions are costly," give two examples from your own experience.

Pass out Guidepost H (page 84).

Ask for their comments and questions about these five marks of a mission. Also ask for what they might add or change.

(Section 7) Reflecting on the session

About 10 minutes
Purpose: To reflect on the session.

Working in pairs, each shares the most significant part of the session and the difference it might make in his/her life. After 5 minutes, ask for three or four to share the most significant part of the session and the difference it might make in his/her life.

(Section 8) Closing and prayer

About 3-5 minutes
Purpose: To remind all of the place and time of the next session.

Remind them of where and when for Session Two. Advise them it will center on a way to find a mission. Ask each to pray in silence for the person on the right. Close with the Lord's prayer.

h

Each mission has five marks

Each mission is centered in love and justice.

Some missions are deeds. Some are words. Some combine deed and word. Without the presence of love or justice, an action fails to be a mission. Will your mission improve the daily lives of the people involved? In our personal lives, we love face-to-face. In our public life, we love by being just.

Missions are specific.

Each mission calls for specifics in what you do or say. A home-builder is on mission to use the design and materials that the client wants and can afford. An elected office-holder is on mission to talk with her constituents as a peer, not as a superior. A teacher is on mission to know his material and to present it clearly.

Missions are costly.

Missions cost in time and energy. Jesus alerted his followers to this fact when He said. "If any want to become my followers, let them deny themselves and take up their cross and follow me" (Mark 8:34).

Making a loving relationship work, parenting with sensitivity, increasing your competence at work, and voting as an informed citizen are costly missions. Missions can call for risk taking as well. A resident taking on a mission to support low-income housing in her neighborhood risks having to cope with the anger of neighbors. A youth leader at his church risks stressing his family by taking time to chaperone a mission trip for the youth group.

Jesus also cautioned his followers when he said, "Foxes have holes, and birds of the air have nests; but the Son of Man has nowhere to lay his head" (Luke 9:58).

Missions can lead to the conflict and pain of confronting and seeking to correct wrongs. A parent takes on his or her teen's anger by repeatedly calling for healthy, life-preserving values over what can be only passing trends. Whistle-blowers can lose their jobs when they tell the truth about some abuse in the system, the business, or the government agency they serve. In such moments, we are tempted to give up confrontation and correction and to withdraw into forgiveness and acceptance of what is as beyond any hope of change. To say to oneself, "Let it be," can be self-protection rather than wisdom.

Missions need God's help.

Our capacity to bring greater love and justice into the world by ourselves is limited. The love or caring that a situation or person needs can drain our energy. Broken people or situations can drain our energy even more quickly. Wrong-doing by people can tax our forgiveness. Further, the best of our intentions and actions can be infected with self-serving or self-righteousness, or both. We need God's help to keep us focused on the needs of others rather than on our own needs.

Missions satisfy us as we share in God's mission.

We see what we are doing bear fruit as love and justice grow. When there is little or no response or progress, we need to trust that God's love or justice will prevail in the long run. Parenting requires patience because the results are long in coming. Social service is slow to bear fruit as well. People in elected office learn to make change one step at a time.

Always, our trust is in God to prevail. Missions carry the special reward of the peace "which surpasses all understanding" (Philippians 4:7) because we trust God to overcome some day.

Historical note

In 1984, the Anglican Consultative Council listed these five marks of mission. The mission of the Church is the mission of Christ:

1. To proclaim the Good News of the Kingdom
2. To teach, baptize and nurture new believers
3. To respond to human need by loving service
4. To transform unjust structures of society, to challenge violence of every kind and pursue peace and reconciliation
5. To strive to safeguard the integrity of creation, and sustain and renew the life of the earth

These five marks are for the church in its actions as an institution. The five marks in this Guidepost apply to the missions of the members in daily life.

5

Session 2 of the Workshop,
*Understanding and Growing as
Missional Members*

This chapter is the second session of the workshop and focuses on the mission discernment form and using it to discern a mission.

(Section 9) Gathering and praying

About 5 minutes
Purpose: Gather and greet one another; and pray for the Spirit.

(Section 10) Getting acquainted with mission discernment forms

About 10-15 minutes
Purpose: to see all seven mission discernment forms and select one to complete.

Pass out Guidepost B (pg. 37).

Leaf through the forms. Note their similarity. (about 2-3 minutes)

Now, each chooses one of these forms for use in the next few sections of this session. Choose on the basis of which mission field interests you the most or challenges you the most. (about 1-2 minutes).

When all have made a choice, pair up to exchange your choice and some of the reasons the chosen field interests or challenges you. (about 4 minutes)

When finished, ask only for a show of hands for which mission fields have been chosen. (about 1-2 minutes)

(Section 11) The pattern of these forms

(About 10-12 minutes)
Purpose: To understand the pattern of these forms.

Pass out Guidepost C (pg. 47).

Ask for three volunteers to help in reading Guidepost C, possibly dividing after "how it is used in this book" and "parent, a competent worker, or an engaged citizen." (3-4 minutes)

Comment that these forms are central for missional members. Therefore, take a few minutes to be sure that you understand the pattern noting, especially, the words in bold. (Allow 2-3 minutes)

Ask for what needs to be clarified and where the pattern is not clear. Answer and invite those who understand the pattern to help. (About 4-5 minutes)

(Section 12) Working with the first two questions of the mission discernment form

About 25-30 minutes
Purpose: to review and to practice ways to work with the first two questions about what God is doing in a mission field and what a goal for life in that field might be.

Pass out Guidepost D (page 50).

Have six participants read the first four paragraphs (through ". . . on the mission discernment form."). You read "Gil's story . . ." through ". . . leading his section." (About 3-4 minutes)

Then seven more volunteers read the seven stories. (About 3-4 minutes)

Now, ask each to fill in the blanks of any one or two of the examples. (Allow 4-5 minutes)

When all have completed at least one, ask them to pair up to share their responses. Then both reflect on what has been learned and questions they may have about this activity. (Allow about 8-9 minutes.)

Now, ask each pair for their learnings and questions they may have at this point. (About 5-7 minutes.)

(Section 13) Each completes a mission discernment form (Guidepost B)

(About 50-70 minutes)

Purpose: to view some guidelines for completing the forms and to allow time for each to complete the mission discernment form each has chosen.

The group reassembles as a whole. Each opens the forms, Guidepost B, to the mission field he or she has chosen.

Pass out Guidepost E (pg. 56).

After handing out Guidepost E, ask for six different volunteers to read the questions; each reads a question or group of questions and the tip connected to it. The italics emphasize the key part or hint of each tip. After each guideline, ask, "Can you see yourself using this guideline?" This is a key question. Be sure all can answer "yes" before moving on to the next question. Read the last four paragraphs yourself.

Note that Chapter 8 is made up of completed mission discernment forms for each mission field. They come from a mix of missional members and offer diverse styles of writing.

Now it's time to complete the form for the mission field of their choice. This usually takes about 15-20 minutes. If asked for help, be direct and answer clearly and briefly. When all requests for help have been met, allow five minutes or so and, then, ask how it's going. Again, be ready to help as requested. Check after 15 minutes are up asking if any need more time. Allow the time that is needed.

When all are finished, ask them to form trios, ideally working with others known less well. Each one shares his or her mission discernment form. The other two make notes of what is unclear; and, with Guidepost E at hand, note what needs to be sharpened to accord with the suggestions in Guidepost E. These notes are shared with the reader; clarification and comments are made as needed. The other two members share their forms one at a time, notes are taken and shared; clarification and comments follow as needed. Advise they will have 15 minutes or so for this sharing.

When each trio has completed their sharing and discussion, ask what are some of your comments about using these forms to find one of your missions. Hear from each trio and each person in each trio. This activity is central and care should be taken that all see themselves able to use these forms from now on. (Allow 10-15 minutes.)

Here are some additional notes about the sharing process:

- If what you share is already familiar to your teammate, your sharing is a useful affirming of the power available to us in church life.
- If your teammate is not a churchgoer, hearing how the church helps you can open the door to a dimension of church life and mission that may be new for him or her.
- Still further, if your teammate is not a church member, a mission is still incomplete until we encourage him or her to explore Jesus' people and his mission.

Close this section commending them for learning to use a key activity of missional membership.

(Section 14) Reflecting on the session and closing

(About 10 minutes)
Purpose: to share reflections on the session.

Ask the following questions:

- What has this session been like for you?
- What helped us make it work?
- What needs to be improved or changed?

Note on the white board or easel the answers to these questions. Add that you will review the comments for cues in your own planning for the next session. Close with a brief prayer of thanksgiving for some hard work done together and for their families or friends who are generously coping with their absence; and a prayer for new insights as they reflect on this session and the previous one. Remind them of the time and place for Session Three.

6

Session 3 of the Workshop,
*Understanding and Growing as
Missional Members*

(Section 15) Gathering and praying

(About 5 minutes)
Purpose: to gather, greet, and pray for the Spirit's help.

Gather and greet one another over refreshments and pray for the Spirit: to lead and to teach us at this time; to guide the congregation we serve; and for us, with God's help, to be part of God's ongoing work to make all of life more loving and more just. Have the overall purpose and goals listed somewhere. Comment that we continue to work on the first four in various ways.

(Section 16) What we have done and what's next

About 5-10 minutes
Purpose: to recall the basic elements of missional membership already covered and to outline the goals for this session.

(a) Recall what we have done:

  • We have defined missional members as members who seek to be on God's mission wherever they are;

- We have identified seven mission fields – home, work, the community, the wider world, leisure, spiritual health, and church life and outreach;
- We have discussed five marks of a mission – centered in love and justice, specific, costly, needing God's help, and satisfying;
- We have examined mission discernment forms; and
- Each of us has chosen and used one of the forms to discern a present mission or one to begin.

Does anyone have any questions about any of these? Invite group members to answer. Be ready to fill in as needed.

(b) Propose four goals for today:

- for each one to discern some of the skills, talents, or gifts one has or will need for the mission discerned in the last session;
- to explore how to change from forming church members to forming missional members;
- to arrive at a mission statement that centers on forming missional members; and
- to consider first steps to carry it out.

Post these four goals and invite any questions for clarification.

(Section 17) Discerning the skills, talents, or gifts you have or will need for your mission

(About 25-30 minutes)
Purpose: To identify the skills, talents, and gifts you have or will need for the mission you have just discerned.

Pass out copies of Guidepost I (pg. 96).

GUIDEPOST

Some of today's skills, talents, and gifts

Skill, talent, or gift	Example
Advocacy	Defending those who cannot defend themselves. *Example: Helping poor children to get the health care they need.*
Coaching skills	Helping others to develop valuable skills *Example: Coaching or helping with a girls' or boys' soccer team*
Communication	Turning thoughts into words that others can understand; and putting them in a way that encourages further discussion. *Example: Discussing issues of the day without having to win.*

Hospitality	Helping others to feel at ease. *Example: Helping church visitors to meet others at coffee hour.*
Imagination	Seeing new possibilities. *Example: A unique idea to help under-achieving youth.*
Intuition	Sensing the needs of others. *Example: Recognizing when a friend needs to talk or needs someone to listen.*
Monitoring	Keeping track of systems or events. *Example: Helpful oversight of others focused on enabling their success, not on criticizing them.*
Organization	Pulling together different parts into a cohesive whole. *Example: Coordinating the work at an auto repair shop.*
Self-knowledge	Understanding your talents and limitations. Example: *Knowing how much energy you can devote to helping others.*

Biblical lists of gifts for your information

Romans 12:6-8: ". . . prophecy, in proportion to faith; ministry, in ministering; the teacher, in teaching; the exhorter, in exhortation; the giver, in generosity; the leader, in diligence; the compassionate, in cheerfulness."

1 Corinthians 12:8-10: ". . . wisdom . . . knowledge . . . faith . . . healing . . . working of miracles . . . prophecy . . . discernment of spirits . . . tongues . . . interpretation of tongues . . ."

Ephesians 4:11: ". . . some apostles, some prophets, some evangelists, some pastors and teachers . . ."

Ephesians 4:12 (a biblical purpose of gifts): ". . . [they are given] to equip the saints for ministry, for building up the body of Christ . . ."

Some good news is that you already have many of the skills, talents, and gifts you will need for your mission. What you need but do not have is asked for in prayer.

Ask the participants to form trios with the usual guide of being with those you know less well.

Some skill, talent, or gift is likely to be involved in each answer to one of the questions on the mission discernment form. Remind them that today's words are being used for skills, talents, or gifts. We will not use the biblical names for gifts as found in Romans 12:6-8, 1 Corinthians 12:8-10, or Ephesians 4:11-12. Those lists from Paul are in a first century framework of church life. We are in the 21st century and use today's words to talk about today's skills, talents, and gifts that are used in all of life.

For some examples, review Guidepost I. Ask them to read the samples and the biblical lists to themselves. Then, ask for comments. Next, ask how comfortable are they with using this approach to skills, talents, and gifts. As best you can, help the cautious to be willing to try it for a time.

Next, in each trio, each of you reads through your mission discernment form. The other two will listen for and jot down a skill, talent, or gift the reader already has or one a listener suspects will be needed. Either of the two listeners may ask the reader to wait for note-making before the next question and answer are read. After Question 8 is read and notes completed, the notes are shared. Where skills, talents, or gifts are needed, one of the two listeners prays briefly for them to be developed, and gives thanks for the gifts already present. Repeat this process for the other two in your trio.

Ask, "What are some of your comments and insights on this way of discerning skills, talents, and gifts?" Next, ask, "As you discern some of today's skills, talents, and gifts, to what extent do you begin to sense a fresh encounter with God's presence or help in your life through listing these skills, talents, and gifts?"

So far, we have laid the foundation for forming missional members as one of our basic purposes. Now, for the big step. How do we make this change?

(Section 18) How church members can become missional members

(About 20 minutes)
Purpose: To explore a way to make the change to forming and supporting missional members as primary.

Pass out Guidepost J.

GUIDEPOST j

Changing from forming church members to forming missional members

Systems theory offers a useful method for changing an organization.

I was introduced to systems theory by Ezra Earl Jones in 1990 when he was serving as the General Secretary of the General Board of Discipleship of the United Methodist Church. Its basics are:

1. a system achieves the results it is designed to achieve;
2. if a system is not achieving the results desired, change the system;
3. introduce a change that will achieve the results desired and redesign the system around it;
4. train all leaders in the change and ask them to introduce it into the parts of the system they lead; and
5. provide a way to maintain the change.

The desired results will begin to appear from the outset; and real change will be apparent in three to five years. [For more information, see *Quest for Quality in the Church: A New Paradigm,* Jones, Ezra Earl, Discipleship Resources, 1993.]

For our church, change can look like this.

(1) We seem to form members who think of mission only as participating in any church-based or church-sponsored activity. While whatever they do Monday to

Saturday may be loving and just and done believing God is helping them to do it, our members tend to believe it falls short of "real mission." This is not the formation we want.

(2) We want to form members for whom all they do with God's help to make the world more loving and just is mission wherever they are and whenever they do it. We need to change our church so that we form our members for mission, to realize the missional members they already are by baptism when they joined God's mission.

(3) Helping our members to discern their missions in each area of daily life will lead to the change we want to make, namely forming our members to know they are always on mission and always to see themselves as missional members. We believe that using mission discernment forms is one way to achieve this change

(4) We will help all leaders to discern their missions in each area of daily life. In turn, they will help all those lead to discern their own daily missions. We will see that all coming for baptism (including, where possible, the parents and godparents of infants and young children), for confirmation or reaffirmation, or for transferring membership receive help to discern their daily missions; and we will include all newcomers, as well. These are "entry points" to becoming missional members. We will use the mission discernment forms to achieve this purpose.

(5) The official board will provide ways to maintain this change for all members to become missional members. Expect real change to be evident in three to five years.

More simply for our church, the five steps are:

(1) we begin to see that our members tend to see only "church work" as missional and what they do Monday to Saturday as just not "good enough" to be called missional;

(2) we want to redesign our church so that our members see all of their daily lives as missional;

(3) we will use the mission discernment forms as tools to form our members as missional members;

(4) we will emphasize helping our leaders to live as missional members so that: they can form those they lead to live as missional members; and they can begin to form all at "entry points" to become missional members; and

(5) we, the official board, will find and use ways to continue forming all members as missional members; and we expect all of these changes to be evident in three to five years.

Guidepost J summarizes a theory of change called systems theory. It will help us to change into forming missional members as a church. Systems theory in its present form appeared in 1950. I did not meet it until the 1990's. I am still relearning it. Keep this guidepost available to you whenever you want to sharpen your understanding of it.

Let's get into Guidepost J by reading it together. We will read it in three sections. Ask someone to read the first section beginning "Systems theory offers . . ." as the rest follow the text. The next section, "For our church . . .," applies this basic outline to our church. Select five people to read the five parts of this section as the rest follow the text. The last section, "More simply . . .," is a simpler version of the outline. Ask five more to read the last section as the rest follow the text.

Next, for 2-3 minutes, reflect in silence on what is unclear and what seems left out that needs to be added. Perhaps, put on newsprint or a whiteboard key words to stimulate their reflection such as unclear, left out, to be added.

After a few minutes, ask for and note what is unclear; what has been left out; and what needs to be added. Ask someone to list the points made on the newsprint or whiteboard. Ask someone else to make notes and distribute them after the workshop. Do not try to edit the text of Guidepost J at this point. The goal is simply for all to see it as a procedure to be worked with as we set about making the change.

Ask if we are ready to go ahead with this plan bearing in mind the comments that have been made. When there is a consensus to go ahead, go to the next step. Suggest they understand consensus to mean each feels heard and understood and is willing to go ahead with the rest even if one's own specific concern is not part of the plan. Consensus means there is a general shared sense of being heard and willing to go ahead with the plan together.

Next, we will draft a working mission statement. I will propose a statement; post it with space for edits or changes; ask you to add your edits and changes; and we will decide whether or not to try it for a year.

We will work for consensus on a statement that is workable enough to try for a year. After a year, we will revisit it for modification or revision, or to drop it and work out a wholly new mission statement. Our actual experience will be our guide to a common-sense decision at that time.

If you believe there is consensus to move ahead on this basis, do so. If not, perhaps set aside the next regularly scheduled meeting to review where we are and decide where to go next.

(Section 19) Drafting a working mission statement for our church

(About 30 minutes)
Purpose: All share in editing or revising a proposed mission statement.

Drafting a working mission statement is not as hard as it sounds. I will propose one and ask that we work together to revise it enough to make it work for all of us.

Remember, we will revise it after the first year; and from then on, every two years in the light of our experience in using it. Constant revision will keep it a "working" mission statement of how we are living together as agents of God's mission day by day.

What are your criteria for a congregation's mission statement? I use two – a theology of missional members and an explicit reference to the mission fields. A way to put my theology of missional members in these pages has five parts.

1. A theology of missional members in this book has five parts.
   (a) God's love and justice have overcome evil, sin, and death in Jesus Christ.
   (b) Jesus Christ's mission in today's world is to overcome evil, sin, and death with the love and justice of God.
   (c) Jesus calls us to join his mission and he shares his power, the Holy Spirit of God's love and justice, with us in our life and work with him.
   (d) We join his mission in baptism and become part of the church among whom we find the guidance and the power to carry on our daily missions.
   (e) The Spirit helps us to discern and to live our missions as part of God's mission.
2. It makes explicit reference to our daily mission fields.

My proposal for our work appears below. All five parts of the theology are implied by its first part – "We are . . . help . . ." This meets the first criterion. My second criterion is met by the second part – "in our homes . . . outreach." We will check the mission statement we develop against these criteria.

Now we get to work on revising the following mission statement:

Living the Mission at Trinity Church
We are part of God's mission to make all of life more loving and more just with God's help in our homes, in our work, in our community, in all of the wider world, in our leisure, in our spirituality, and in our church's life and outreach.

Post the draft mission statement for all to see. After a few minutes of silent reflection, ask for their edits, revisions or additions. Write down their suggestions. Work this way for 15 minutes and see where you are; take more time if it is needed.

When you sense a level of satisfaction with the changes made, check that the two criteria mentioned above are either present or implied. If they are, ask if we might next move on to planning how to use it. Congratulate everyone on the significant work they've accomplished.

(Section 20) Reflecting on the session

(About 5-10 minutes)
Purpose: To reflect on what helped or hindered our work during this session.

Please form into trios with those you still need to know better. Discuss: what are some of the more important developments or ideas of this session? and what parts of this session need more work?

One trio at a time, ask for and list the responses to these questions for use in further planning.

We move next into some needed activity. Section 21 will get us started.

(Section 21) Planning for living, and reflecting on a mission

(About 15-20 minutes)
Purpose: Planning to live the mission discerned in Session 2, and anticipating first steps in living our church's mission as just put together in this session.

Knowing the full structure of missional membership, it is time to practice living a mission. Begin the practice with living the mission discerned in Session 2.

Set the date of the next session two to three weeks from this session. Optimum is for the date to be the date of the next official board meeting. Selecting some first steps in living our mission as a church is, indeed, work of the official board. Therefore, designate this meeting as an official board meeting whether or not it is in the cycle of official meetings.

Each one opens the mission discernment form (Guidepost B, pg. 37), completed in Session 2 and focuses on the mission discerned in Question 5. Each decides if there is time before the next meeting to, at least, start the mission discerned in Session 2. If you need to revise your mission to be able to start it before the next meeting, revise it quickly now. Next, note when you will start the mission; what you will do or say or both to get it started; how you will make notes on the response to your start; what follows as the contact develops; and where each of you is as the contact ends. Also, be ready to note any ways that you sense God might be at work as you live this mission.

Form trios. One by one, each shares his or her mission and its field, when and how the mission will be started, how notes will be made of the response, what follows as the contact develops, and how notes will be made of where each of you is as the contact ends. Each clarifies as requested.

Allow about 10-15 minutes for this sharing – and more if needed.

Each trio reports about each of the missions chosen including the field involved.

Close with a sharing of comments on what themes seem to run through the missions named.

(Section 22) Closing prayer

(About 5 minutes)

Holding hands each prays in silence for the mission of the person on the right and then the person on the left. Close with the Lord's Prayer. Remind all of the next meeting noting that it is a regular official board meeting – another way to lock in the permanence of what has been accomplished in the workshop.

7

Session 4 of the Workshop,
*Understanding and Growing as
Missional Members*

In This Chapter

This chapter is the fourth session of the workshop. It centers on sharing experiences in living the mission each discerned in Session 2, and on choosing first steps to implement the congregation's mission as discerned in Session 3.

(Section 23) Gathering and praying

(About 5 minutes)

Purpose: To greet each other and to prepare for sharing about our lived missions and for planning first steps to implement our congregation's mission statement.

Gather and greet one another over refreshments. Pray for: careful sharing of experiences and learnings from living the missions discerned in Session 2; careful listening to the experiences and learnings being shared; and being open to sensing God, Jesus, or the Spirit at work in the experiences and learnings perceived in living our missions and sharing about them.

(Section 24) Sharing experiences and learnings from living a mission

(About 60 minutes)

Purpose: To share experiences and learnings from living the missions discerned in Session 2 and begin to sharpen our sense of God, Jesus, or the Spirit at work as we live our missions.

112

We have completed a thorough encounter with the procedures and concepts of missional membership. Each of us has
just tested its heart – discerning and living a mission in one
of our mission fields. How has it gone? What have we
learned? To share, form trios with those you know less well.

Within each trio, have each person share their experience in living their mission in these six steps. Fill in the
blanks to help the sharing be concise. Take 2-3 minutes to fill
in the blanks; give each person a double-spaced worksheet
with these questions:

1. Name the mission field and your mission.

2. When and how did you start?

3. What was the response? Be as specific as you can.

4. How did the contact develop?

5. Where were you when the contact ended; where did you
   sense the other was as the contact ended?

6. What sense, if any, did you have of God, Jesus, or the
   Spirit at work as you lived this mission?

Once all have completed their notes, begin the sharing (about 4-6 minutes per person). The first person shares his or her story slowly so the others can take notes as desired and pauses as requested for clarification. The other two share in the same manner.

When all three have shared, they discuss what they are learning about God's, Jesus', and the Spirit's presence and work in us. This sharing can become very exciting. Let the excitement flow.

Observe each group with care. When sharing is relatively complete, ask each trio to list two or three of the major learnings that have emerged. Then, ask for the two or three major leanings that appear to be shared by all. (Expect about 5-10 minutes for this sharing by the whole group.)

Move on commenting that we have shared experiences and learnings from living our missions. By now, I pray, we have a fairly full experience of and feeling for missional membership. We now proceed to some specific ways to implement our mission statement for missional membership.

(Section 25) Next steps with the mission statement

Purpose: To plan how we will start to use this mission statement.

Pass out Guidepost K.

GUIDEPOST

k

Next steps with the mission statement

Mission statements have to be used to work. Next steps for us have three parts:

- what I might do as your minister;
- what we, I as your minister and you as the official board, might do; and
- what we as a congregation might do.

My next steps might be:

- to preach a series of sermons and teachings on being missional members;
- to see that our mission statement appears on our Sunday handouts and our publications;
- to see that our Sunday prayers, the Prayers of the People or the Pastor's Prayer, include prayers for our mission fields that rotate among the seven mission fields week by week; and
- to begin, in various ways, to use the mission discernment forms to prepare adults and youth for baptism or confirmation, to prepare the parents and godparents of young children for baptism, and to orient to missional membership those who are new members by transfer or by choosing to make us their worshiping community.

Together, as pastor and official board, we might:

- reflect on this workshop at our next regular meeting as to what it meant to each of us and any unresolved issues it raised;
- complete and discuss, at our next four meetings, our mission discernment forms for home, work, the community, and the wider world;
- reflect on the effect of these four meetings on us individually and as a group;
- commit ourselves to complete and to discuss at the three meetings following these four the last three mission discernment forms for leisure, spiritual health, and church life and outreach;
- see that all signs on the premises and inside the buildings reflect missional membership – e.g., on the church hall, "Meeting about our missions;" on the church office, "Supporting our missions;" in the sanctuary, "Praying about our missions" or "Feeding our missions;" etc. (change them as our experience and imagination suggest);
- see all of our publications – Sunday bulletins and handouts, packets for visitors and newcomers, newsletters, stationery, and the like – carry the mission statement; and
- see that our newspaper notices and street signs carry a brief form of our mission statement such as "Part of God's mission for a more loving and just world."

As a congregation, we might:

- help each organization and task force to review its purpose and activities to align them with being part of God's mission for a more loving and just world;
- begin to tell our friends, both church and nonchurch, about our mission statement and how we feel about it;
- tell regional meetings of our communion about our mission statement and what it means and what it is doing for us; and, above all,
- live as lovingly and justly as we can in each mission field each day with God's help.

Ask each of four to read one of the four paragraphs of Guidepost K. In pairs for the next five minutes, discuss what needs to be added, deleted, clarified, or changed. Ask for and list their comments one pair at a time. Plan to revise Guidepost K as needed using this list.

At the next meeting of your official board, offer an easy way to select two starting points from each of the three lists. For example, allow time for each to select three items from each of the three lists. Record their choices. As a group, discuss and select which two from each list will be your starting points. Go on to plan how to start each of the selections.

Thank everyone for working hard during these four sessions.

(Section 26) Reflecting on the four sessions of the workshop

(About 15 minutes)
Purpose: To list reflections on the four sessions of the workshop; and to acknowledge God's presence and help throughout the workshop.

Ask the whole group to discuss:

- what helped our work together?
- what hindered out work together?
- suggestions for next use of this workshop.

Use your own pattern for ending prayers; perhaps, try this one.

1. Hold hands.
2. Acknowledge God's presence and help throughout the session and the whole workshop.
3. Have each individual pray in silence for the person on the right; and, then, for the person on the left.
4. Invite special prayers from anyone.
5. Say the Lord's Prayer.

6. Give a final blessing: "The grace of our Lord Jesus Christ, . . ." or any favorite.

8

How Seven Missional Members
Discerned Their Missions

It is time to share with you sample full mission discernment forms of seven individuals who are seeking a mission in one of the mission fields. Two principles guided them. First, to stay with the facts of each situation. Second, to follow the directions of Guidepost E (pg. 56), be sure to mention:

1. what God, Jesus, or the Spirit have been doing;
2. how you want life to be in this mission field;
3. what you are doing now to achieve this goal;
4. what you still need to do;
5. what, specifically, you will do or say and when you will do or say it;
6. who can help you to do or say it;
7. how will you describe what you will do or say as part of God's mission; and
8. how you will suggest the church might help.

Look for how each appears in each form.

Home (a current mission or one I will begin)

Eric's mission in his home

1. **What has God been doing in or telling me about my life at home (includes all life in my home and**

**life with my close friends)? Where is love or jus-
tice at work or needed? What message am I getting about it? I will try beginning with something
like: "I believe God is . . ."**

I believe God is calling me to reconnect with my larger
family. At a wedding celebration for my cousin and her
partner, a second cousin grabbed me and said: "Let's or-
ganize a reunion. Will you join me?" I have time available
in my semi-retirement, and I want to be intentional in
connecting with my family and forming or deepening relationships with family members.

2. **As I think about God's message, what is my vision
   or goal for how I want my life to be at home?**

I have spent years seeking to understand my extended
family. Learning to give them space in which to find their
own resources is a way in which I want to grow in trusting
God's power.

3. **What am I doing right now to make this vision or
   goal a reality?**

We are gathering a reunion for this summer. Now I want
to open up a conversation about how we want to spend
our time together. I want this to be "our" event, not mine.

4. **What do I still need to do? I will begin with
   thinking of where I need to bring or to increase
   caring or love, fairness or justice. I will take into
   account my skills, talents, gifts, limitations, and
   convictions.**

I need to be particularly aware of reaching out to those
who seem most distant.

5. **What, specifically, will I do or continue to do to make my vision or goal a reality and when will I do it? I will limit myself to just one action in word or deed or both. As I choose this action, I am discerning my mission in my home.**

   My mission is to connect more deeply with these relatives in order to know them better. I've already started.

6. **Who can work with me to carry out this mission? How will I describe the mission to interest him or her? My answer with the person's name and words I might actually use.**

   I have support in a group that will help to hold me accountable, with whom I will spend some time forming the questions I have and seeing that I tend to the members who are the least natural for me to connect with.

7. **When the time is right and with permission, how can I explain how what we are doing is or can be part of God's mission? How will I ask if he or she is comfortable with my sense of my life at home as part of God's mission? My answer with words I might actually use.**

   I see this as directly related to the work of God; making friends is one of the favorite paraphrases of 'reconciliation' that I have heard.

8. **When the time is right and with permission, how could I encourage my teammate to turn to the church for help and support? I will begin with how the church helps me; that may give me an idea of what to suggest for how it might help him or her. My answer with words I might actually use.**

"Conversation about church stirs up strong feelings for family members. Does it do that for any of you?"

Work (a current mission or one I will begin)

Lisa's mission at work

1. **What has God been doing in or telling me about my work (includes home management, school, and volunteer work)? Where is love or justice at work or needed? What message am I getting about it? I will try to begin with something like: "I believe God is . . ."**

   I believe God is encouraging me to have my team take on bigger and more complex projects for the good of those suffering from chronic illness in my work as a manager for a national non-profit organization.

2. **As I think about God's message, what is my vision or goal for how I want my life to be at work?**

   I will be doing more and better work for those who need it, especially those coming from a low socio-economic background.

3. **What am I doing right now to make this vision or goal a reality?**

   I am writing multiple complicated funding requests.

4. **What do I still need to do? I will begin with thinking of where I need to bring or to increase caring or love, fairness or justice. I will take into**

account my skills, talents, gifts, limitations, and convictions.

I need to bring in more partners so we can work together to bring this vision to reality.

5. **What specifically will I do or continue to do to make my vision or goal a reality and when will I do it? I will limit myself to just one action in deed or word or both. As I choose this action, I am discerning my mission in my work.**

I will confer with people and organizations this week who can further this important work.

6. **Who can work with me to carry out this mission? How will I describe my mission at work to interest him or her? How will I ask for the other's help? My answer with the person's name and words I might actually use:**

My specific partners are, as yet, undefined. However, I will be calling universities and public health professionals to identify key and willing partners.

7. **When the time is right and with permission, how can I explain how what we are doing is or can be part of God's mission in my work? How will I ask if he or she is comfortable with my sense of my work as part of God's mission? My answer with words I might actually use:**

This work is a calling and I sense everyone working in it also senses that.

8. **When the time is right and with permission, how could I encourage my teammate to turn to the**

church for help and support? I will begin with how the church helps me; that may give me an idea of what to suggest for how it might help him or her. How will I ask if he or she has ever thought of the church as helping in this way? My answer with words I might actually use:

I have mentioned to at least one partner that I ran a recent program at my church to help low socio-economic level parents and caregivers and that can be an opening that I might build on to mention the connection between my faith and beliefs and the work I do.

Community (a current mission or one I will begin)

Mac's mission in his community

1. **What has God been doing in or telling me about my life in my community (my neighborhood, town, or city)? Where is love or justice at work or needed? What message am I getting about it? I will try beginning with something like: "I believe God is . . ."**

I believe I am getting the message that we need to be less business-like; to remember our ultimate purpose is bringing people together; to work at connectivity, my word for it; and to have the joy of living better.

2. **As I think about God's message, what is my vision or goal for how I want my life to be in my community?**

If we get connectivity right, everyone will feel included; I will feel a part of the gas station people when I drive up. It's all part of connectivity.

3. **What am I doing right now to make this vision or goal a reality?**

After some time on the board, I realize I am not there to make decisions; I am there to make sure everyone has input; then, we make better decisions. Even if people do not get their own way, they are satisfied they gave their input. There is less conflict and more cooperation.

4. **What do I still need to do? I will begin with thinking of where I need to bring or to increase caring or love, fairness or justice. I will take into account my skills, talents, gifts, limitations, and convictions.**

I need to bring to the front how decisions and views can impact vulnerable people; for example, decisions about taxes or views about what life should be like.

5. **What specifically will I do or continue to do to make my vision or goal a reality and when will I do it? I will limit myself to just one action in deed or word or both. As I choose this action, I am discerning my mission in my community.**

When making decisions, I will slow down wanting to "get things done" so that we stop and think about the bigger picture and concentrate on being 100% present to the moment we are in.

6. **Who can work with me to carry out this mission? How will I describe the mission to interest him or her? How will I ask for the other's help? My an-**

swer with the person's name and words I might
actually use:

I will talk with my wife, Millie, about our slower decision-
making so that we can hear from more people and ask if
she thinks it will work.

7. **When the time is right and with permission, how
can I explain how what we are doing is or can be
part of God's mission? How will I ask if he or she
is comfortable with my sense of my life in the
community as part of God's mission? My answer
with words I might actually use:**

I will ask my wife, "Millie, when I work this way, I have
an inner peace that comes from somewhere beyond me.
Does that make any sense to you?"

8. **When the time is right and with permission, how
could I encourage my teammate to turn to the
church for help and support? I will begin with
how the church helps me; that may give me an
idea of what to suggest for how it might help him
or her. How will I ask if he or she has ever thought
of the church as helping in this way? My answer
with words I might actually use:**

I will ask my teammate, "Church helps that sense of won-
der about the inner peace coming from somewhere.
Sometimes I think of it as the Spirit working in me. Does
that kind of thing ever happen to you?"

Wider World (a current mission or one I will begin)

John's mission in the wider world

1. **What has God been doing in or telling me about my life in the society, culture, economy, government, or environment of the county, state, nation, or world? Where is love or justice at work or needed? What message am I getting about it? I will try beginning with something like: "I believe God is..."**

   I believe the Spirit wants me to continue going to meetings of the county committee of the party I belong to.

2. **As I think about God's message, what is my vision or goal for how I want my life to be in the wider world?**

   I want to see that our county committee discusses current issues in the county, the state, and the nation taking love and justice, caring and being fair, as our guiding principles.

3. **What am I doing right now to make this vision or goal a reality?**

   For the next meeting, I am planning how to ask who will work with our county and state candidates for election in November as they prepare their positions on the issues before their respective offices.

4. **What do I still need to do? I will begin with thinking of where I need to bring or to increase caring or love, fairness or justice. I will take into account my skills, talents, gifts, limitations, and convictions.**

I need to check out my thinking with a colleague on our town committee.

5. **What, specifically, will I do or continue to do to make my vision or goal a reality and when will I do it? I will limit myself to just one action in deed or word or both. As I choose this action, I am discerning my mission in the wider world.**

At the next county meeting, I will ask who is working with our candidates as they prepare their positions on the issues the people they represent face.

6. **Who can work with me to carry out this mission? How will I describe the mission to interest him or her? How will I ask for the other's help? My answer with the person's name and words I might actually use:**

[This is August. The primaries have just settled who the candidates are. The next county meeting is in September.] "Bart, can I treat you to a cup of coffee to get your reactions to what I want to say at the next county meeting." [If he agrees and we are talking over coffee, I might talk this way.] "Tell me what you think. I want to speak up at the next meeting asking who is working with our candidates as they prepare their positions on the issues they will face? How shall I put it? Is there anyone I should talk with about this?"

7. **When the time is right and with permission, how will I explain how what we are doing is or can be part of God's mission? How will I ask if he or she is comfortable my sense of my life in the wider world as part of God's mission? My answer with words I might actually use:**

"Bart, can I take a couple of minutes for some church talk. [If he says 'yes,' I will continue.] The big word for me is 'mission.' I believe God is on mission working for a more loving and just world, a more caring and fair world. So, in whatever ways that work, I want to see our candidates take positions on questions that mean something. One of them is, of course, affordable housing. So, how do I do it and who do I ask for help?"

8. **When the time is right and with permission, how could I encourage my teammate to turn to the church for help and support? I will begin with how the church helps me; that may give me an idea of what to suggest for how it might help him or her. How will I ask if he or she has ever thought of the church as helping in this way? My answer with words I might actually use:**

"Bart, can I share what church means to me? I don't know how much church is in your thinking. For me, church is the place that keeps reminding me that caring and being fair, being loving and just, have to come first—even in politics. That's what church stands for, for me. Have you ever thought of church that way?"

Leisure (a current mission or one I will begin)

Veronica's mission in her leisure

1. **What has God been doing in or telling me about my leisure time (includes any activity that rests or refreshes me)? Where is love or justice at work or needed? What message am I getting about it? I will try beginning with something like: "I believe God is . . ."**

I work hard as a prison chaplain for the state and serve as priest-in-charge at a nearby Episcopal Church. The Lord has been asking me to refresh myself. In prayer, I have recalled biking and enjoying the scenery. Now in the Adirondacks, I will learn the bike trails and enjoy the beautiful mountains.

2. **As I think about God's message, what is my vision or goal for how I want my life to be in my leisure time?**

My vision is to allow time for biking, to take along my Bible for reading, and to share this with others.

3. **What am I doing right now to make this vision or goal a reality?**

As I recover from a foot injury, I will window shop for a new bike. I have finally found one and can't wait to pick it up.

4. **What do I still need to do? I will begin with thinking of where I need to bring or to increase caring or love, fairness or justice. I will take into account my skills, talents, gifts, limitations, and convictions.**

I need to focus on my health, to purchase the bike, and get the safety equipment I need. I will study the bike trails. I look forward to connecting with other bikers and increasing my care for the Lord's creation.

5. **What specifically will I do or continue to do to make my vision or goal a reality and when will I do it? I will limit myself to just one action in deed**

or word or both. As I choose this action, I am discerning my mission in my leisure.

I will continue to shop for that bike.

6. **Who can work with me to carry out this mission? How will I describe the mission to interest him or her? How will I ask for the other's help? My answer with the person's name and words I might actually use:**

My husband has said he would help and even join me. I will say, "Janos, I have shared how I used to bike in New York City. I want to start biking again. What do you think about it and would you like to join me some time?"

7. **When the time is right and with permission, how can I explain how what we are doing is or can be part of God's mission? How will I ask if he or she is comfortable with my sense of biking as part of God's mission? My answer with words I might actually use:**

We are called to rest and have time for leisure. This is time for communion with the Lord and time for fellowship with my brothers and sisters.

8. **When the time is right and with permission, how could I encourage my teammate to turn to the church for help and support? I will begin with how the church helps me; that may give me an idea of what to suggest for how it might help him or her. How will I ask if he or she has ever thought of the church as helping in this way? My answer with words I might actually use:**

The church has encouraged and supported me in taking some time off. Once on the road and having a good sense of the bike trails, I can ask others if they have ever thought the church would help them with encouragement and support for taking and enjoying leisure time.

Spiritual health (a current mission or one I will begin)

Josh's mission for his own spiritual health

1. **What has God been doing in or saying to me about my spiritual health (my inner life with God and any activity to meet my spiritual needs)? Where are either love or justice or both at work or needed? What message am I getting about it? I will try beginning with something like: "I believe God is . . ."**

   I believe God is alive in people, so through their expressions of love God is present and communicating with me. The message I'm getting is that people have the power within them to make life better every day, but it is about the choices we make. Stifling love or letting other emotions and forces be dominant leads to unhealthy choices. I want to be guided by love so God's message can be expressed through me.

2. **As I think about God's message, what is my vision or goal for what I want for my spiritual health?**

   I don't actively care for my health right now very much other than by making responsible choices. My goal is to become healthier and to build upon healthy habits that I already have and to create new ones. This includes continuing to participate in our church community and to care for others in whatever way I can.

3. What am I doing right now to make this vision or goal a reality?

I attempt to be thoughtful and responsible. I don't think most things are all that complicated. I basically just try to do what I think is right based upon all the information I have and the time that I have.

4. What do I still need to do? I will begin with thinking of where I need to bring or to increase caring or love, fairness or justice. I will take into account my skills, talents, gifts, limitations, and convictions.

There is so much more that I could do to be part of more goodness in the world. I feel like I am constantly stretching already. Being more loving comes to mind as something that will keep me stretching in a positive way. I think I could also be a little more lighthearted, but a seriousness generated by a sense of responsibility has always driven me and that seriousness is sometimes in conflict with lightheartedness.

5. What specifically will I do or continue to do to make my vision or goal a reality and when will I do it? I will limit myself to just one action indeed or word or both. As I choose this action, I am discerning my mission for my spiritual health.

The one action that I will apply to multiple people in my life is to schedule structured time to spend with people who I care deeply about.

6. **Who can work with me to carry out this mission? How will I describe the mission to interest him or her? How will I ask for the other's help? My answer with the person's name and words I might actually use:**

I will schedule time to spend multiple days in a row engaged in healthy experiences with each of my parents separately, my wife, each of my children separately, and specific friends. The time spent will focus on creating a connection between us through the shared experience that we're having, and that will help us to have an even stronger foundation to do the important and good stuff we must do in our lives both separately and together, as well as to face any difficult times ahead together.

7. **When the time is right and with permission, how can I explain how what we are doing is or can be part of God's mission? How will I ask if he or she can agree with my sense of my spiritual health as part of God's mission? My answer with words I might actually use is:**

While spending focused time with each person, I will inquire about what matters to them, what gives them a sense of purpose, and what fulfills them. I expect that what I'll hear is their personal mission, even if we don't use that language.

8. **When the time is right and with permission, how could I encourage my teammate to turn to the church for help and support? I will begin with how the church helps me in my spiritual life; that may give me an idea of what to suggest about how it might help him or her. How will I ask if he or she has ever thought of the church as helping in**

this way? My answer with words I might actually use is:

I think I will be able to ask each person where/what they think their sense of purpose came from, or how they developed it. Did they learn it from family, school, church, friends, stories they read, heard, or watched, doing volunteer work, etc.? I could ask what resources they will turn to over time to help them stay focused on the things that matter most.

Church life and outreach (a current mission or one I will begin)

Helen's mission in the church

1. **What has God been doing in or saying to me about my church's life and its outreach in service and evangelism and calling others to join Jesus' mission; or in the life of my district, diocese, or communion in the United States. or worldwide church; or in interchurch or interfaith activities? Where are either love or justice or both at work or needed? What message am I getting about it? Try beginning with something like: "I believe God is . . ."**

   I believe God is telling me my work with Sunday School and youth is very important. Even though my children have aged out of Sunday School, I feel strongly that the work I do is very important to the life of our church. Young children in worship give new life to the church.

2. **As I think about God's message, what is my vision or goal for how I want to participate in my church's life and outreach?**

I want to keep the children and youth engaged in worship and learning in a number of different ways. Christian education does not happen just on Sundays between 10:00 and 11:00 AM but in homes, on youth trips to help and to learn from people in need such as in Puerto Rico and Maine, and in our Sunday evening programs for children and youth.

3. **What am I doing right now to make this vision or goal a reality?**

I am a support person for the pastor and Christian Education Coordinator with their great ideas and visions for how to make things better for our children and youth.

4. **What do I still need to do? I will begin with thinking of where I need to bring or to increase caring or love, fairness or justice. I will take into account my skills, talents, gifts, limitations, and convictions.**

I want to help our children and youth to continue to read scripture and translate it into their daily lives; to care for themselves and for others; to provide for the food shelf, our school, and shut-ins; to keep church a safe place to talk about whatever they want to talk about; and to be good stewards at church and in our environment.

5. **What specifically will I do or continue to do to make my vision or goal a reality and when will I do it? I limit myself to just one action in deed or word or both. As I choose this action, I am discerning my mission in my church's life and outreach.**

I will continue to support the pastor and Christian Education Coordinator in building an experience for children and youth where they like to be here and to be learning and growing as Christians.

6. **Who can work with me to carry out this mission? How will I describe the mission to interest him or her? How will I ask for the other's help? My answer with the person's name and words I might actually use is:**

Our pastor, our Christian Education coordinator, our Christian Education committee, and all of our volunteers work with me to carry out this mission. We interest others by making all of our activities open; non-members can test the waters and try us out bit by bit. Our youth program is The (name of town) Youth Project and has drawn in others beginning with the first youth mission trips.

7. **When the time is right and with permission, how can I explain how what we are doing is or can be part of God's mission? How will I ask if he or she can agree with my sense of supporting the pastor and CE Coordinator in building an experience for children and youth where they like to be here and to be learning and growing as Christians as part of God's mission? My answer with words I might actually use is:**

We talk about our work with the children and youth as what we are meant to do; it is something we believe we have to do. I share that, even though my own children have outgrown much of our children's program, I feel like the children and youth are mine.

8. **When the time is right and with permission, how could I encourage my teammate to turn to the**

church for help and support? I will begin with how the church helps me in my life at church; that may give me an idea of what to suggest about how it might help him or her. How will I ask if he or she has ever thought of the church as helping in this way? My answer with words I might actually use is:

For those on the edge, all of what we do is open and has drawn in non-members to come and decide for themselves. For us who are already involved, it is time to think together about our dreams and visions and to develop our sense or statement of purpose or mission.

9

Spreading Missional Membership

Spreading missional membership takes three steps:

First, the team spreads the missional member vision among the members of the congregation as individuals and as church leadership teams.
Second, the congregation finds a mission in the community or region it serves.
Third, the congregation develops ways to support the missions of the members in the wider world.

Special note: Directions in the previous pages were direct and specific; the next pages provide ideas with the choice of which to use up to you and your team.

The pastor and the board are the team that will spread missional membership throughout the congregation. They will help the congregation find a mission in the community or region it serves, and they will help the congregation develop ways to support the missions of the members in the wider world. There are three steps to spreading missional membership in a church.

I. The Congregation Learns to Live as Missional Members

The first step is to consider the best time to present members of the congregation with being missional members. Be guided by reaching the most with what you judge to be most essential in the time you think you need and can ask for and get. And think afresh about times – e.g., Sunday at coffee hour, Sunday brunch and meeting, and the like. The session's actual length depends on the options you choose to include. Length, when, where, and how often to meet are your choice.

A potential roadmap for introducing the congregation to missional membership

<u>Purpose:</u> to understand living as missional members and to build commitment for the church to grow in living this way.

Essential for the opening conversation with congregational members are numbers 1 and 2 from the seven-point roadmap proposed below. Create a plan for talking to others, guided by specific items on the roadmap; always include #6, which involves the mission discernment forms.

1. **Pastor and some board members tell how they became excited about missional membership.**

2. **What has been done so far; the church has been guided by our two principles of mission and the mission statement developed in Section 19.**

    God is on mission to make the world more loving and more just. We join God's mission to make the world more loving and more just with God's help.

    [The mission statement developed in Section 19, pg. 105-107]

3. **An activity to build awareness of living with seven mission fields.**

Use Guidepost A to build awareness of living with seven mission fields. Follow the activity with how we came to talk of seven mission fields. Use Guidepost L for biblical examples of seven mission fields.

For practice in thinking of seven mission fields, ask the participants to recall some of their favorite biblical passages and ask for the mission field involved in each passage cited. Some passages like the feeding of the five thousand (Mark 6:30-44) may have more than one field involved.

4. **How we came to talk of seven mission fields.**

Perhaps, share the mission discernment forms for home and work as a tested means for discovering your missions. Pass out and discuss Guidepost C as a resource for completing the forms. For samples of completed forms pass out Eric's form for a home mission and Lisa's form for a mission at work. Have a packet of the other five forms available for those who may want to work out all of their missions now.

5. **Five marks of a mission.**

Share and discuss Guidepost H, "Five marks of a mission."

Advise them of mission discernment groups. Offered regularly, groups of three to eight or so meeting with one or two of the board for coaching usually follow these steps.

a. Meet to get acquainted, agree on a procedure (e.g. do all seven or do the first four – home to wider world, take some time off, and re-group to do the other three), and receive the first form and

Guidepost C to be completed at home for the next meeting.

b. The next and following meetings discuss the form for the week guided by the boldface words in Guidepost C. Some groups become so excited by this sharing of the mission for the week that they promise to live their new mission during the week and report the outcome at the next meeting. During the reporting at the next meeting, a coach asks often, "Were you aware of God or the Spirit helping you?" The reporter and the rest become quite excited with each "yes" and how it was experienced.

c. The meetings continue until all seven mission fields have been covered.

Invite questions and announce when the next such group will be offered.

When you close, mention some of the ways being missional members will begin to show up in church life. Perhaps, cite the mission statement being included in all publications; signs and ads describing the church as "Part of God's mission for a more loving and just world;" one of the seven mission fields is prayed for every Sunday; and in all preaching and teaching.

6. Mission discernment forms and on-going mission discernment groups.

Hand out and explain the forms for home and work. Guidepost C will help. Note its basic points. Comment that completing these forms is a skill developed in mission discernment groups that are offered regularly. Encourage each member to join such a group.

Now practice the form for home or the form for work. Pass out Eric's completed form for home and Lisa's completed form for work. After quick reads of both, each individual chooses either home or work to complete.

Allow about 5-7 minutes for each to complete the form chosen. Ask for two or three to share what they have written. Then, ask for comments on the forms. Finally, ask if any were surprised at how easily they found this way to talk of God's work in their lives. Close with announcing the next group to practice completing all of the forms.

7. Evaluation and moving on together.

Asking these three questions can be enough.

    a. In what ways did this session help you to understand being missional members?

    b. What questions about being missional members still need to be answered?

    c. How ready are you to move ahead with learning about being a missional member?

GUIDEPOST L

Biblical examples of our seven mission fields

The seven daily mission fields by title:

- **home** (includes all life in the home and life with close friends)
- **work** (includes home management, school, and volunteer work)
- **community** (neighborhood, town, or city)
- **wider world** (all from social norms to voluntary, business, or governmental systems)
- **leisure** (whatever rests or refreshes you)
- **spiritual health** (your inner life with God)
- **church life and outreach** (your part in your church's life and outreach at any level)

Some examples of the seven fields in the Bible:

- **Home.** The *home* life of Ruth leads her to choose to stay with Naomi and become an ancestor of David (Ruth 1:15-18 and 4:13-17).
- **Work.** Needing to support himself in Corinth, Paul resumes his skill as a tent-maker to *work* with Aquila, already a tent-maker, and becomes both a friend and co-worker with Aquila and his wife, Priscilla, in spreading the Gospel (Acts 18:1-3 and Romans 16:3).
- **Community.** In spite of fierce opposition within and without, Nehemiah led the rebuilding of the walls and gates of the vulnerable, remnant *community* of Jews in

Jerusalem and he did it in fifty-two days (Nehemiah 6:15-16).

- **Wider world.** Exploitation of the poor called Micah, the prophet, to challenge Israel to "do justice and to love mercy" in the *wider world* of the nation's way of life (Micah 6:8).
- **Leisure.** Stories of mission in *leisure* time are found in the many accounts of Jesus dining with others (e.g., Mark 2:1-4).
- **Spiritual health.** The Syro-Phoenician woman provides us with an example of someone who will go to great lengths to secure the *spiritual well-being* of others (Mark 7:24-30).
- **Church life and outreach.** The *church life and outreach* of the first Christians drew others in through the quality of their shared life together (Acts 2:43-47).

Some overall norms to keep for all that missional members do in their church's life and outreach

Time in the activities and committees of their church is only part of their full involvement in the life and work of their church. Here are seven norms for whatever missional members do in their church. Publish them regularly. Discuss them in successful times as well as in problem times. Add to them as experiences suggest.

1. Participation in worship
2. Prayer and biblical reflection as individuals and in groups
3. Growth in understanding Christian life and faith
4. Sharing in activities of Christian fellowship and community
5. Leading when asked
6. Sharing in the maintenance of the facilities and programs
7. Contributing to the financial support of the congregation

II. Your church's organizations join the church's mission statement

The second step is for the church's organizations to join the church's mission statement. Each organization in the church–committee, group, or task force–needs to know its mission and how it participates in the church's mission. A pair of the team members schedules a time with each organization. Where the organization does not have a mission statement, schedule a meeting with it to develop a mission statement for it. A suggested plan for such a meeting follows:

1. Prayer for mutual understanding and for guidance.
2. List all of the activities of the organization.
3. Brainstorm a broad purpose or mission statement that can include all of the activities.
4. Review the church's mission statement.
5. Brainstorm a rewording of the organization's purpose so that it reflects the church's mission statement in one or more ways.

If an organization already has a stated purpose or mission statement, you can use steps #4 and #5. Do have both the organization's purpose and the church's mission statement posted. To illustrate, five samples of what organizations might do follow. Note too, the mission field served appears in parentheses.

Worship Committee/Altar Guild
(Church life and outreach)

Activities
- Prepare the altar and credence table for communion or other special liturgies.
- Preserve and lay out vestments for officiants.
- Change hangings to fit the season of the church year.
- Maintain sanctuary/worship area for.

Mission statement: With God's help, our mission is to encourage and to deepen the spiritual experience of all worshipers.

Hospitality team (Church life and outreach)

Activities
- Prepares for coffee hour, serves, and cleans up after worship on Sunday.
- Prepares refreshments, serves, and cleans up for receptions after funerals.

Mission statement: With God's help, our mission is to encourage friendship and mutual support among worshipers.

Youth program (Community)

Activities
- Develop an understanding of youth needs both within the church and the surrounding community
- Plan for programs and services to meet the identified needs of youth
- Create a plan to welcome youth both within the church and the community
- Help youth grow in faith within the supportive church framework

Mission statement: With God' help, our mission is to meet the needs of youth, welcome them to the church family, and help them grow in faith.

Men's group (Church life and outreach)

Activities
- Meet monthly for breakfast supplied by one of the members with 30 minutes for informal conversation and an hour for each to share his current ups and downs.
- Gospel for the week opens the hour and prayer closes it.

Mission statement: With God's help, we affirm each other and keep a standard of confidentiality.

Annual bazaar (Church life and outreach)

Activities

- Collect and prepare desirable items for a one-day sale.
- Invite the whole community and welcome warmly all who come.
- Oversee and clean up after sale with proceeds to the church.

Mission statement: With God's help, to sell our handiwork reasonably, make known that our church is open to all, and to aid the church budget.

III. A congregation finds a mission in the community or region it serves

The third stage of spreading missional membership occurs when the congregation develops ways to support the missions of the members in the wider world. One question the congregation can ask itself is, what is the community or region your church serves?

For example, I was an active priest of an Episcopal Church in Montvale, New Jersey. The small town of Montvale had three churches, which grouped easily with the churches and temple of the neighboring towns of Park Ridge, Woodcliff Lake, and Riverdale. These towns and a few others are called the Pascack Valley region, named for the small brook they shared. The Pascack Valley region in turn is part of Bergen County, one of the most populous counties in the state.

Serving Bergen County was too large an area, so the church I served began with recognizing each member of the churches and temple as on mission in the Pascack Valley.

It is important to embrace the members already on their own community missions.

- Some serve on or go to meetings of the land use committees of their community.
- Some serve on the school boards or the committees of parents or guardians who meet non-budget needs of the classes of their children or youth.
- Many are the cherished good neighbors to whomever lives next door.

Your church needs to be known as a loving, justice-seeking friend of its community. How will your church find out where love or justice are needed and take up meeting that need?

In 1968, five churches (Catholic, Episcopal, Lutheran, Methodist, and United) and one temple (Beth Sholom) in Montvale and Park Ridge, NJ organized the Pascack Valley Center (PVC) to serve the community.

A team of four PVC members interviewed people in education, health, business, government, voluntary associations, and religion. Asking, "What are the needs of people in your network?," they collated the results and started with offering rides for people without cars.

Response was slow so the PVC went on to the needs of youth in danger of getting into trouble with the police. Using New Jersey's method of Juvenile Conference Committees, they set up such a committee for Montvale as a starting point. It worked well as long as leadership for it from the PVC lasted.

The PVC continued with helping to start a senior housing residence in nearby Westwood, NJ in the 1980's, and now is part of Meals on Wheels for northeast Bergen County.

However, it is important to remember that as needed as the PVC may be, it is the members of the Pascack Valley churches and temple and their individual missions who are the primary agents of mission for that area.

An example of a congregation supporting the missions of its members in the wider world

One church found a way to support the mission of living in the wider world by holding monthly sessions of "Practicing God-talk" during coffee hour. The offering was built around research that found most adults continued their education through their own, individual reading of all kinds.

The education planners further perceived that their members would probably benefit from reading and discussing issues in the wider world. They found a way to help interested individual members in three stages: finding reliable commentators on an issue; analyzing that issue with the help of such commentators; and articulating possible solutions with the help of such commentators. In addition to putting worthwhile reading in more hands, this approach reflected much of the congregation's teaching about any instances of love or justice as places where God's loving and justice-centered Spirit are present and active.

So, interested leaders looked for articles in magazines and newspapers for members to read on their own and discuss in a small group on fourth Sundays during coffee hour. The articles chosen came from all areas of life in the wider world such as education, health, the income gap, politics, government, economics, conservation, and climate change. Publishing the article and its theme well in advance and making the article available for advance reading allowed members to participate or not as they chose. Links to the articles were published for individual follow-up. Attendance ranged from two or three to seven or eight with usually that number of articles being picked up by individual members for their own reading on their own time. Here are three random samples of the articles.

- "Matthew Desmond Talks about the Church's Response to Housing Instability," an interview with the Pulitzer-winning author of *Evicted: Poverty and Profit in the American City*, by Betsy Shirley from *Sojourners*, June

2017. Read a summary of this article on-line or print it out at http://bit.ly/2hlQF7t.
- "Can the Graduation Approach Help to End Extreme Poverty?" by Tony Sheldon, in Yale Insights, February 7, 2017. Read it or print it out at http://bit.ly/2odDlEx.
- "Selling the Protected Area Myth" by Richard Conniff, a contributing opinion writer, in *The New York Times*, 6/10/18. Read the artcle: https://nyti.ms/2JG1pqY.

At the fourth Sunday sessions, the leader needed only to ask for comments on the article shared for lively discussion to follow. While not the whole answer to preparing members to find and live their missions in the wider world, it was indeed an approach open to all of the members.

10

The Spirit and Missional Members

Some of this chapter's premises

- Spirituality begins with asking how to live and, once answered, goes on to ask for power to live that way.
- We find God in any part of life by looking for love or justice there.
- We talk freely of spirits today—school spirit, national spirit—so Spirit with a capital S for the Holy Spirit becomes an easy way to talk about God too.
- Begin spiritual experience by asking where is God— where are love or justice—part of my life today.

Why is spirituality important?

What makes the difference between someone who walks with Jesus, and someone who gives up? A person's spirituality makes the difference. When you are rooted in God, you hang in there and, like Simon and Andrew and James and John, you follow when Jesus says, "Follow me" (Mark 1:16-20). That's why this chapter on spirituality is so important for missional members. How strong is your spirituality? Where or in what or in whom do you place your trust for help and for direction?

In these pages, spirituality means the practice of communicating with God – in particular, seeking God's help for guidance in how to live your missions and for power to – actually – live them.

For Christians, the good news is that God both guides us in discerning our missions and empowers us to live our missions. Many come to Jesus for love, forgiveness, and new life. Come to Jesus to learn how to live and to receive power to live that way.

How to find God?

How then does one find God? Find God by looking for love or justice in your life and in the world around you. Wherever you find love or justice, you are finding God because love and justice are the characteristic works of God.

Devotional materials and retreats also can help you find God. Looking for the presence of love or justice, of caring and being fair, will always work. These pages are full of such stories. That electrician discussed earlier had met God through his grandmother's care to teach him to do the right thing. The parents, owners of a neighborhood "quick stop" for food and household items, were seeking baptism for their son, 8, and their daughter, 6. During the session of preparation for the baptism, all four looked closely at how they were making life more loving and just. As the session ended, the father said to his wife, "You know what this means. This means we have to start going to church." As noted above, they became regular worshipers and the mother taught Sunday School and served on the board as she continued her work at the post office delivering mail.

The Holy Spirit, the Spirit, and missional members

Among the many forms and practices of spirituality is a sense of communicating with God – of listening to and talking with God. Missional member living begins here. The first question to discover a mission is: "What has God been doing in or saying to me about my life (at/in a mission field)? Where are either love or justice or both at work or needed? What message am I getting about it? I will try beginning with: "I believe God is . . ." The Holy Spirit enables communication with God of missional members.

I recall again my theology professor in seminary who defined the Holy Spirit as God at work in the world. Working from this succinct phrase, I have come to speak or write of the Holy Spirit as the Spirit with a capital "S." To talk of God as Spirit is an easy way to talk of God in today's world. We are at home with talk of "team spirit," "my spirit," and "the spirit of the time." These spirits are quite real even though they cannot be seen, heard, felt, smelled, or tasted. The Spirit's usual works are some forms of love or justice. They too are real even though they cannot be seen, heard, felt, smelled, or tasted. "Spirit" helps us to bridge the gap between the world of daily life and the world of faith. We talk of the Spirit helping us to pray and the spirit of a company that helps its workers to avoid shoddy work.

Some ways missional members meet the Spirit

Story 1

My prayer time has come to be a time of sensing communication with the Spirit. I begin with the scripture reading for the day, reflect on it, and pray in the context of the mission field in rotation for that day. I end with a prayer or action for the day. I note the prayer or action and begin the next day's prayer time recalling that prayer or action and looking for any answers to the prayer or actions that occurred during that day. I am constantly thankful to find the prayer answered in some way or the action taken effective in some unexpected way. The action taken and the prayer offered were more received than thought up by me. I am finding the Spirit leading me to the prayer offered and the answer that followed is, in the Spirit's own way, a gift from beyond me. The power and wisdom to accomplish the action that had emerged are also a gift from beyond.

Story 2

A group of six met recently to practice using the mission discernment forms. After the first meeting, each session opened with sharing how each participant had lived his or her mission that week. From the second session on, high excitement was the norm. Each had found help from beyond to carry out his or her mission. Weekly, the Spirit had led each to a mission – of what to do about a specific concern; and each week each participant sensed he or she had received help from beyond – from the Spirit – to do what each had sensed was a mission.

Where missional member living begins

Missional member living begins with asking what has God been doing in my life. I remember that a teacher had said, "The Holy Spirit is God at work in the world." How do I find God at work? Wherever I see love or justice, God is there working to make that part of the world more loving or more just. Other forces or people are there at work too, of course.

God was working for a time when the Holy Spirit – or simply, Spirit – would be found by all of us. Joel understood God saying, "I will pour out my spirit on all flesh; your sons and your daughters shall prophesy, your old men shall dream dreams, and your young men shall see visions" (Joel 2:28).

The Spirit had come to individuals – to David, to Elijah, to Isaiah – for their specific missions. Joel understood the

Spirit would be poured out on all. Pentecost and the early church were times of the pouring out of the Spirit on all.

The pouring out of the Spirit makes missional membership possible. Called by the Spirit, missional members discern the Spirit at work in every part of their lives helping them to carry on their missions. Like the disciples who had been sent forth on mission, today's members on mission end a day surprised at how much they have done and inspired by the help they had received to do what they had done. They are like parents delighted to find they can talk with their teenagers, and like members of Congress who rejoice that they can enact laws that really help their constituents.

God's Spirit helps us to see what God wants us to do; then God's Spirit helps us to do it. This book has become my own day by day journey with the Spirit. To perceive where the book needs to go next and then to be able to go there is one of my stories with the Spirit.

Missional members are cautious as they work with others

Missional members work with any for whom caring and being fair, loving, and just, are primary values. While love and justice are primary for many, a certain caution is needed. Many who claim to be loving and just actually have exclusivist views and habits of which they are not aware and for which they need to be constantly on the alert to avoid. None of us is perfect. Each of us needs to be on guard for exclusivist habits and commitments that need to be avoided whenever they arise. With caution we team up with others and expect them to call us to account whenever we are narrow or prejudiced. Likewise, we accept our own responsibility to call teammates to account when they are narrow or prejudiced.

Missional members work with any from other faiths

Missional members work with any of other faiths for whom a more loving and just world are primary. The media are full of stories of such people. The story of Malala is such a story.

Malala Yousafzai was born July 12, 1997, to a Pashtun family in northwest Pakistan. Her father was part of a family running a chain of schools for girls in the region. In 2014, she received a Nobel Peace Prize for her advocacy for education for women and girls. She began her advocacy at age 11-12 with a blog under a pseudonym for the BBC detailing her life during the Taliban occupation of her region. On October 9, 2012 at 15, she was the victim of an assassination attempt. A bullet pierced her left eye and left through her skull. Recovering in hospitals in Pakistan and Birmingham, England, she resumed her advocacy for education for women and girls. Was she a Christian? No. Was she part of the Spirit's work for a more loving and just world? Yes.

The Pascack Valley Center was an interfaith community service in Bergen County in northeastern New Jersey. With some members of the church in Montvale, I started the center in the late 1960s. It was sponsored by four Protestant churches, a Catholic church, and the Jewish temple. The first donation to the PVC came from the temple at one of the organizing meetings the week before Christmas. One of its projects was a planning day for the eighteen towns in the county in the early 1970s. Its participants were the eighteen mayors of the towns, many of whom commented this was the first time they had ever met each other.

Missional members and people of no faith

Paul Tillich (*The Dynamics of Faith*, Harper One, 1956) opened the way for both people of faith and people of no faith to work together for a better world. Tillich's gift was to offer that everyone – believer and non-believer alike – has some ultimate concern that guides their decisions, sustains them as reliable, and promises them fulfilment. One's ultimate concern may be success, one's nation, reason, or science. Since none of these can be proved beyond doubt, maintaining faith in them and following them takes courage. Christians have the same need for courage. Therefore, missional members meet and work with any for whom love and justice are primary.

As an example, Milt, 25 and a missional member of his church, was preparing to take over the family farm. However, climate change was making that future impossible. He reasoned that his years of maintaining farm equipment would give him a leg up on learning the trade of auto repair. His uncle ran an auto repair shop and had a reputation for being caring and fair with both customers and employees. As for church, his uncle, having spent childhood and teen years as a church member, had dropped out of church life and, now, when asked, said only that he had a faith of his own. In his shop today, people bringing a car for repair received a diagram of the work needed with an estimated cost; then they decided about having the repair made there or to go elsewhere. As for the employees, his uncle had a reputation for being a generous and thoughtful owner. It was said that he had kept his people on full pay during the Covid-19 crisis even though business was down by half. His uncle accepted Milt's request for a job and Milt began his career in auto repair there – and carried on his missional member living.

Next steps with the Spirit

The missional member vision evokes still more questions for future chapters of books. Here are some starting points.

- The Spirit is at work in everyone.
- Explore the need for justice as well as love in every part of life

- Christians see the Spirit at work in any faith where love and justice are central.
- Whatever other faiths call love and justice, Christians see as the work of the Spirit, God's Holy Spirit.
- We speak of love and justice lived by non-believers as the work of the Spirit.
- We do not ask other faiths or people of no faith to use our word Spirit for their words or actions of love or justice.
- We find this a most attractive and most open way to live and work with everyone.

Always keep moving with the Spirit

- Expect to be challenged to keep learning about the Spirit.
- These challenges are part of being missional members.
- Never forget you are part of God's mission.
- Count on the Spirit for ongoing help.
- As part of God's mission, turn to any of us for help at any time.

Living our missions

The Spirit is exciting to think, write, and talk, about. However, what really counts is doing our missions. The Spirit is individually experienced and known with the most power when we live our missions!

"And remember, I am with you always to the end of the age" (Matthew 28:20).

Lord Jesus, keep walking with us. Amen.